THE STRANGER'S CONFLICT

Waging the war within

෨

Brad Church

Table of Contents

ca

Table of Contents i

Acknowledgements iii

Introduction vi

CHAPTER 1
Questions...1

CHAPTER 2
Our Human Make-up...18

CHAPTER 3
Aftermath of One Choice 37

CHAPTER 4
A History of Corruption 46

CHAPTER 5
God's Plan to Redeem 65

CHAPTER 6
Restored in Three Phases 78

CHAPTER 7
The Underlying Conflict 87

CHAPTER 8
This, Is War.......................................101

CHAPTER 9
Answers 121

CHAPTER 10

On Moving Forward..134

About the Author 159

Notes...162

Acknowledgements

ᘒ

WHILE THIS WORK IS A result of years of studying and living and has been influenced by numerous people in my sphere of influence, there are a few people I would be negligent if I did not publicly acknowledge their influence in my life.

First, my mother, Margery, who taught the Sunday School class where I first came to faith in Christ at the age of six. She always included Jesus in our holiday celebrations. Her questions have challenged me to dig deeper to find answers. Her life has challenged me to broaden my perspective. The resulting searches have deepened and strengthened my faith.

My wife, Valli, whose perseverance in physical suffering amazes me. I would not want to repeat the trials we have been through in just over 11 years of marriage, but they have made us stronger.

The two men I consider my two best friends in life, Greg and Rick. Greg was my adopted brother, in spirit, as we were growing up. His influence on me, especially in high school, was more crucial than he knows. I treasure the time we have shared as we have reconnected in our lives the past few years.

I met Rick when I went to Bible College in Los Angeles. We studied together, roomed together, laughed together and grew together. We started a business after college. Another friend of mine has used the term, "Foxhole buddy" to describe one of his friends. Rick is my foxhole buddy. Rick is one who read this manuscript early on and provided much needed encouragement and perspective.

Bethany, who also read this manuscript early on. Her feedback and encouragement were also valuable to my continuing on to get this book published and in your hands.

Several pastors have been there at key times of my life. Pastor Jack Oliver, who led me in the baptism in the Holy Spirit. Charles (Chip) Whitman, who was my pastor as I was making the decision to move to Los Angeles and go to Bible College. Pastors Ed and Ivy Stanton, whose radical love and steadfast examples God used to save me from a path of self-destruction and despair. They gave me the space and opportunity to find who I was made to be in Christ. The fact that Ed gave me the opportunity to teach was instrumental in the production of this book – and hopefully, more to come.

Lastly, my PDX Simple Church family, whose acceptance, love and support have meant the world to me and my family these last 13 years. They are truly a unique family of people who have created a community of support and encouragement like none other I have known.

v

Introduction

CR

THE STRANGER'S CONFLICT IS THE product of my own journey of discovery. The book began with feeling frustrated in my relationship with Christ. My frustration centered around two statements made by the Apostle Paul in his letter to the church in Rome which inspired me ask a series of questions. All discovery begins with questions. God is not threatened by our questions as we seek understanding. The Bible clearly teaches that seeking wisdom is a good thing. Proverbs 2:1-5 says:

> My [child], if you receive my words,
> And treasure my commands within
> you,
> ² So that you incline your ear to
> wisdom,
> And apply your heart to
> understanding;
> ³ Yes, if you cry out for discernment,
> And lift up your voice for
> understanding,
> ⁴ If you seek her as silver,
> And search for her as for hidden
> treasures;
> ⁵ Then you will understand the fear of
> the Lord,
> And find the knowledge of God.

Clearly, God is okay with our seeking understand, with our pursuing wisdom, with our asking questions. Questions lead us to discovery.

My journey of discovery began with a simple desire to understand how we, as believers in Christ, are to accomplish Paul's direction in Romans 8:13 to "put to death the deeds of the body" (KJV). I had read that phrase and others like it, for years and came to a point in my efforts to live as a Christian that I frequently felt like I was trying to nail Jell-O to a tree. I was at a loss to know how to do what Paul was charging us to do. I was certain Paul was not instructing us on a masochistic, monastic lifestyle, but it was not totally clear to me how we are to accomplish that which clearly is beyond our human ability to perform.

Here is another thought that was a curious thing to me. The Apostle Paul wrote about a third of our New Testament. He evangelized much of the known, Roman world in his time. He was an Apostle's Apostle. His visions and insight seem to have only been exceeded by his zeal and hard work. Yet, here is what he says about his own struggle. "For what I am doing, I do not understand. For what I will to do, that I do not practice; but what I hate, that I do.[1] So if Paul struggled with this concept of crucifying the deeds of his flesh, don't you think you and I might struggle with it too? Be honest. How do we reconcile God's commands to be holy with this constant inner struggle with doing right? My hope is that as you read, even study, the content of *The Stranger's Conflict* you will gain insight and encouragement.

Every human being who has ever lived has experienced an inner struggle with doing what is right and not doing that which is wrong. Even non-religious people experience this conflict. Here are some simple examples. If you have ever known you shouldn't eat that chocolate cake and eaten it anyway, you have experienced the struggle. If you have known you should go for a run, but made an excuse not to do it, you have lived the struggle. If you've ever thought you should call your mother, or father, or friend and not done it, you have experienced the conflict. And that is not even the stuff that deals with morality. If you have ever seen something you wanted and were tempted to take it without paying for it and didn't do it, you have lived the conflict. If you have ever been tempted to taint the truth with a "white" lie, you lived the conflict. If you have ever had the opportunity to be with a person other than your significant other and walked away, you have lived the conflict. The inner conflict is something we all deal with daily.

When a person comes to faith in Christ, the conflict intensifies. There is a reason for that, which we will talk about later. The truth is, all of us face these issues every day. Some of them are little issues that have little consequence to ourselves or others. Some of these conflicts revolve around issues that will determine the course of our lives for years to come. It is easy to sit back and point an accusatory finger at others. It is quite another thing to look at ourselves and honestly deal with our own issues.

As I was reading one day, Paul's command to put to death the deeds of the flesh, or of the sin nature, caused me to realize how little I understood what he was talking about. I understood the doctrine behind the command, but it was the practical aspect of carrying out that charge that left me baffled. For years, I sat in church, or read my Bible and nodded my acceptance of these words of Paul's out of sheer habit. But I had to stop and ask myself, "What are these deeds of the flesh Paul is talking about?" As a person who first came to faith in Christ at around age six, I have read and reread the following passage more times than I can remember. The New King James version of Galatians 5:19-21 reads:

> *"19 Now the works of the flesh are evident, which are: adultery, fornication, uncleanness, lewdness, 20 idolatry, sorcery, hatred, contentions, jealousies, outbursts of wrath, selfish ambitions, dissensions, heresies, 21 envy, murders, drunkenness, revelries, and the like;" NKJV*

There are a lot of words in there that may not be easily understood in today's culture. I encourage you to pick up a concordance and do a little study of what those words mean. As a believer in Jesus, it is easy to simply smile and nod in agreement when we read a passage like this, or hear it preached in church. That's where I was when I began the quest for understanding. Perhaps you can relate. Here are the same verses in The Message. This version

ix

might help us get a clearer picture of what Paul is saying.

"It is obvious what kind of life develops out of trying to get your own way all the time: repetitive, loveless, cheap sex; a stinking accumulation of mental and emotional garbage; frenzied and joyless grabs for happiness; trinket gods; magic-show religion; paranoid loneliness; cutthroat competition; all-consuming-yet-never-satisfied wants; a brutal temper; an impotence to love or be loved; divided homes and divided lives; small-minded and lopsided pursuits; the vicious habit of depersonalizing everyone into a rival; uncontrolled and uncontrollable addictions; ugly parodies of community. I could go on." The Message

There is some strong language in that passage, isn't there? I submit to you that the works of the flesh are not just sexual sins, or murder, or theft; but the deeds of flesh get down to our attitudes and motivations. Are we harboring anger toward someone? Jesus said that is the root of murder. I suggest that the deeds of the flesh are anything that does not proceed out of loving God with all our heart and loving our neighbor as ourselves. It is a tall order God lays at our feet. It can be perplexing how we are to accomplish it. It is clear to me that the issue is more ingrained in our lives than we realize. Yet, God does not leave us without hope.

You might be wondering why I would call the book *The Stranger's Conflict*? The author of Hebrews wrote, concerning the earliest men and women of faith in the Old Testament, that they considered themselves strangers and pilgrims on the earth.[2] As people of faith in our Creator, we are unique in our perspective of life. We don't see things the same way others do. We are, according to scripture, Strangers here – citizens of another country that is not of this world. Being a Stranger begins with recognizing that, once we come to faith in Christ, our citizenship is in heaven (Philippians 3:20). We are no longer just citizens of this world. We are in the world, but not of the world (John 15:18-19; John 17:16). Because we are now citizens of a different country, a kingdom really, in God's eyes we are His ambassadors here. We are representatives of His kingdom on earth.[3]

Peter echoed this thought in his letter to Christians in the first century. In 1 Peter 2:11 he writes, "Dear friends, I urge you, as foreigners and exiles, to abstain from sinful desires, which wage war against your soul" (NIV). In verses 4 – 10 of chapter two, Peter shares how we are the unique people of God through faith in Jesus Christ. It is the power released in our lives through that simple faith that changes us, that changes our citizenship.

Because we are citizens of another kingdom, we are involved in a conflict with the spiritual forces of this world. Peter mentioned it in the verse above, as did Paul in chapter 6 verses 11-13 of his letter to the Ephesians. There, he wrote about our need to take on the full armor of God because our battle is not a physical one but a battle against spiritual powers in this world. The original reader would have pictured a Roman soldier outfitted for battle. The armor is a vivid picture of a personal battle – a conflict if you will. The Roman soldier was a killing machine. They were outfitted for one purpose – to win battles. Paul's picture is clear: we are engaged in a conflict for which we need to be prepared.

What qualifies me to write this book? Honestly, I have wondered that myself. All I can tell you is that I sensed a persistent prompting to write the book. For me, that usually means God is giving me a direction. I am simply doing my best to obey. Aside from that spiritual inspiration, I was asked to teach at my church a few years ago. What I felt I was to teach that night, was the starting point for this book. The teaching was well received, and I enjoyed myself immensely. Both the teaching and the book were born out of years of study, listening to and watching more mature believers than myself. My own personal experiences with Christ played a large part in this book too.

When I was in my early 20s, I heard God's call to go to Bible College. In 1980, I left my job and home in Portland, Oregon and moved to Los Angeles, California. There was no doubt in my mind, or heart, that I was to move and earn my bachelor's degree in Bible. I chose to minor in biblical languages. While I did not have a job or place to live lined up before I moved, within 48 hours of being in California, I had a job at the college and a place to live with two, great roommates. While I have never entered ministry as a profession, I spent the last 35 plus years studying and living a life of faith in Jesus Christ. The training I received in understanding and studying the Bible has literally saved my life.

After I graduated from Bible College in 1985, I went to work in the secular world, having been thoroughly discouraged from entering full time ministry. I eventually went into business with a good friend from Bible College. We operated that business for nearly three years together. Rick and I remain friends to this day. He and I share both triumphs and defeats; great joys and deep, gut wrenching challenges.

After moving back to Oregon in 1996, I completed a second bachelor's degree in business management. Since then, I have added about 30 graduate level credits to my formal education. Aside from the sense of God's calling to write, I have spent a lifetime purposely learning.

During my career, I have done everything from moving irrigation pipe, to holding a key position on a management team that established and ran a world class distribution operation. I have held positions in warehousing, operations, process improvement, or quality analysis for most of the last 35 years. I am currently a business analyst, researching and resolving business challenges every day.

Operations personnel are charged with creating and implementing solutions for situations and conditions that cause failures. Effective quality and process improvement training teaches us to ask, "Why?" until we get to the root cause of a quality or process failure. Sometimes the root cause is found after a couple of whys. Other times, we must ask ten, fifteen, or even twenty times before we discover the root of the issue. What I discovered in scripture, as I applied that process of analysis to the idea of putting to death the deeds of the flesh, resulted in this book. As I applied that process to my walk of faith, I realized how little I really understood and how much I simply nodded at in agreement.

My search began with one question turning into multiple questions as I read, re-read and re-read yet again the stories of people of faith and their writings recorded throughout the Bible. My quest for the root of the issue led me all the way back to Genesis – to the very beginning of the record of Creator God and his human creations. What I discovered there, I found consistently illustrated throughout the history of the nation God chose to be His people. If the story ended here, there would be no hope for much of a future for us individually, nor for the family of humanity. Our fate would be sealed.

Thankfully, our Creator is full of love and compassion. His plan to save human beings from the destruction they chose for themselves begins to unfold with the call of Abram in Genesis 12.

Roughly 2,000 years later, Jesus was born in Bethlehem and secured a solution for humanity. But if the incarnation, life, death, resurrection and ascension of Jesus Christ secured a solution for human beings, why did Paul feel the need to tell us to put to death the deeds of the body? You see? More questions.

I have opted, for the most part, to use end notes for scripture references. In some chapters, I use or quote over 40 scriptures. I felt that to insert the reference every time in the text would be distracting. All the scripture I use is referenced with a superscript number, like this.[21] The notes for each chapter are at the end of the book.

It is my hope that the work that follows will be as beneficial to you in reading it, as it has been to me in writing it. There are many subjects touched upon in the book that I did not delve into more deeply because this is not meant to be a deep, theological investigation of different subjects. The focus of the book is to answer the primary question, "How do you and I crucify the deeds of the flesh?" While writing the book, I got sidetracked on several issues, but deleted much of the content of those side trips because I felt pressed by the Spirit to keep this work focused on the question at hand. To the best of my ability, I have stayed true to the message of the book – the assignment that the Holy Spirit gave to me. I hope the reading of The Stranger's Conflict blesses you and helps you gain understanding of how to live in this world as a citizen of heaven. It is my prayer that you strive to deepen your relationship with our Creator and Savior and, thereby, live at peace with our Creator.

CHAPTER 1

Questions

ༀ

*"7 Ask and it will be given to you; seek
and you will find; knock and it will be
opened to you. 8 For everyone who
asks receives and he who seeks finds
and to him who knocks it will be
opened. Matthew 7:7-8*

WHEN WE ASK QUESTIONS, WE discover. If there is
no question burning in our hearts and minds
begging to be answered, we likely won't discover
anything. We simply will not be motivated to
search for an answer. My hope is that, by the end of
this chapter, you will be asking questions like I did
when I started the process that led to this book.
God loves a person who genuinely seeks truth. Our
questions do not intimidate God. In fact, He loves
when we ask with a desire to know and
understand. After all, He is the One who said,
"Seek and you will find."[1] So I encourage you to
open your mind to ask questions in a genuine
pursuit of God's truth.

In this chapter, we will discuss three scenes from
the life of Jesus. They involve a series of
interactions with the religious leaders of Jesus' day,
a comparison of Manna and Jesus and Jesus'
transfiguration on Mount Herman and a
subsequent confrontation with a demon. Like many

believers, I have read these sections of the Gospels numerous times. During a recent reading of the New Testament, these events caused me to ask some questions that led me on a journey for answers. What I discovered has forever changed my view of life as a Stranger.

Controversy with Jewish leaders - John 7 - 8

Throughout Jesus' ministry, he experienced confrontation with the Jewish leaders. No section of the New Testament provides a clearer picture of that than John chapters 7-8. In these two chapters, we see a series of events that occurred during the Jewish Feast of Tabernacles. The animosity and jealousy of the Jewish leaders toward Jesus had been building since He started His public ministry. Their hatred of Him reached a fever pitch in this first section of scripture we will review now.

The Feast of Tabernacles took place in the late summer to early fall. It was a weeklong festival that commemorated Israel's journey from Egypt to Canaan – from bondage to freedom – and was a time for the Jews to give thanks to God for the productivity of the new land. It was one of the major festivals of the Jewish calendar. Jews from all over the world would come to Jerusalem to celebrate the festival. For some, it was an annual trek. For others, it was a once in a lifetime journey. Many in the crowds that heard Jesus teach were not from Jerusalem but represented the inhabitants of the known world. When they went home, they shared about the things they saw and heard in Jerusalem. The news of Jesus would have been a major topic of discussion as these travelers returned home.

This was the time for the Jewish leaders, the teachers of the Law and the Pharisees, to shine. They put on their best show for the Jews who came from near and far. The last thing they wanted was someone publicly challenging their authority and practices, as Jesus did.

Jesus' usual custom was to teach in the areas where worshipers gathered around the Temple. This not only gave Him access to the crowds, it exposed him to the Jewish leaders, the Pharisees, Sadducees and teachers of the Law. At this point in his ministry, the Jewish leaders were looking for Jesus and the crowds were talking about Him.[2] Halfway through the festival, Jesus walked in among the crowd and began to teach.[3]

The Jewish leaders' hatred of Jesus centered on three areas: What He taught, that He healed on the Sabbath and who He is.

The Jewish leaders taught not only the law of Moses, but thousands of statutes Jesus referred to as the "traditions of men"[4] or simply as "traditions".[5] These traditions were rules the religious leaders added to the Law of Moses through the centuries since the nation returned from the Babylonian captivity. Presumably, these rules were to bring greater understanding of how to live out the law, but they only served to confuse the issue of living in a relationship with God. They also supported a religious system that fed the pride and increased the power of the religious leaders.

In contrast to the Jewish leaders, Jesus taught only what He had been told by His Father,[6] that He comes from the Father and that He knows the Father. Jesus exposed the traditions of men and taught a purer faith. Jesus expresses the root of His teaching in Matthew 22:36:40. It was the heart of the Law of Moses, "Love the Lord your God with all your heart, with your entire mind and with all your strength and love your neighbor as yourself."

Regarding healing on the Sabbath, the Jews were adamant about not doing work on the Sabbath.[7] The idea of Sabbath went back to Creation when God rested from his work on the seventh day.[8] Likewise in the Law, God directed Moses to give the people one day in seven to rest.[9] When God gave the Israelites manna in the wilderness, He did not provide it on the Sabbath, but required them to gather two days of manna the day before the Sabbath. Ordinarily, the manna would decay if they gathered more than they needed for one day. But for the Sabbath, they were to gather an extra ration and it did not spoil. God supernaturally provided a day of rest for His people as they wandered in the wilderness for forty years.[10]

God so cared for His people, He wanted to give them a day of rest. He knows we need it. The fact that God preserved the Manna that was gathered in obedience, but the same Manna would decay if

4

gathered in disobedience is a testimony to God's desire to be active in every aspect of the lives of his people. Even the seemingly mundane, day-to-day things like gathering food. God has not changed. He still desires to be actively involved in all areas of our lives.

Because Jesus healed on the Sabbath, the Jewish leaders saw this as work and a violation of the Sabbath law.[11] However, Jesus called them out and asked that if they had a sheep fall into a ditch on the Sabbath, would they not pull it out? How much more should a son or daughter of Abraham be set free on the Sabbath?[12]

Jesus also taught that the Son of Man is Lord of the Sabbath.[13] In other words, the Sabbath is meant to be a day of rest, refreshment and enjoyment. It is not meant to be a day that we are stifled by religious burdens. The Sabbath was created for us, not the other way around.

The third issue of controversy was who Jesus is. This is by far the most volatile issue Jesus had with the Pharisees. Jesus was not universally accepted or rejected. The crowd was split, as were the leaders. John 7:31, 40-41 states many believed in him. Nowhere does scripture say all the people believed, nor does it say no one believed. There was always a mixture of people who believed and did not believe. Even among the Jewish leaders there was dissent, however cautious it may have been. In verses 7:51-52, Nicodemus posed an objection about condemning Jesus without giving Him a chance to explain who He is. Nicodemus was rebuffed by those who said there is no prophet who comes out of Galilee. It was this Nicodemus who came to Jesus late one night to ask him questions.[14] He came late at night because to be seen being in favor of Jesus would put him in danger of rejection by his peers.

The disputes Jesus encountered with the leaders went on during several days of the festival. These disputes culminated in John 8:48-59 over Jesus' claims as to who stood before them. The Jews, who did not believe Jesus was the Messiah, continued to press him. Jesus responded by raising the issue of the eternal life he provides through obedience to His word. The Jews said, "Abraham died and so did the prophets, yet you say that whoever obeys your word will never taste death. Are you greater than our father Abraham? He died and so did the prophets. Who do you think you are?"[15]

Jesus responded by saying that He does not glorify himself, but His father glorifies him. Further, he stated that, "Your father Abraham rejoiced at the thought of seeing my day; he saw it and was glad."[16]

The Jewish leaders scoffed at Him. They said He was demon possessed, that He wasn't yet fifty years old and there was no way He could have known Abraham, nor could Abraham have known Him.[17] Jesus' response to the leaders in John 8:58 rattled their cage like no one had before.

*"Very truly I tell you,"Jesus
began. "before Abraham was born, I
am!"*

All through this dispute with the Jews, Jesus had
been talking about His Father, where He had come
from and what validated His ministry. But when
Jesus said this, He was claiming to be the very God
who delivered Israel from Egypt. He was claiming
to be the One, True, Creator, God! In no uncertain
terms, with no hidden meanings, no veiled
references, with this one statement, Jesus laid down
the gauntlet. He said, "I am God, who has delivered
you and whom you claim to serve." Their response
was to pick up stones to kill Him, but Jesus slipped
away because it was not yet His time.[18]

Questions: How could those who were supposed
to be the educated guides and leaders of Israel –
those who had knowledge of the scriptures and
supposedly the relationship with God – how could
they not see the truth in what Jesus was saying?
What made these teachers of the Law so closed to
the possibility of Jesus being the Messiah? Most of
them appear to have not even considered it a
possibility. It would have been a simple inquiry to
discover that, though Jesus was from Galilee, He
was born in Bethlehem. The Messiah was to come
from Bethlehem.[19] It seems the leaders were more
interested in finding ways to discredit Jesus rather
than discovering whether He was telling the truth.
Why? If Jesus was the Messiah as He claimed,
would that not be ultimately good for the Jewish
leaders?

7

Many have observed the Jewish leaders were jealous and fearful that their prestige before the people would be damaged. They may also have feared the Romans who were constantly on guard for rebellion among the Jews. Certainly, as Jesus confronted the leaders and denounced them as hypocrites and empty tombs,[20] they would have become defensive and enraged. While all these observations are true, there is something deeper that lies behind their reactions to Jesus and their desire to eliminate Him. It is the reason behind the reason. It is what we discover when we keep asking "Why" until we get to the root.

Jesus - The Bread of Life - John 6

John Chapter 6 starts out with a great crowd following Jesus because He had done many miracles of healing and deliverance from demons among them.[21] While many people were seeking healing, there were others who were there simply to see the show.

As the crowds came to Him late one day, Jesus asked Philip, "Where shall we buy bread for these people to eat?" Philip's response portrays how overwhelming the situation was. "It would take more than a half year's wages to buy enough bread for each one to have a bite!"[22] The human need in the situation was simply beyond their ability to meet in a traditional way.

8

Have you been overwhelmed by life's circumstances? You are not alone. Jesus gave the disciples an assignment they could not fulfill on their own. Then He did an amazing thing, He showed Himself to be sufficient for what they needed to fulfill the assignment.

Andrew found a boy with five small barley loaves and two small fish. Not only were the resources few in number, they were small in size. Jesus gave thanks for what they had. As they distributed the loaves and fishes, they multiplied and there was enough for all to eat.[23] Imagine, breaking the bread and pulling the fish apart, expecting it to diminish as it is broken and watching as it multiplied and fed thousands. The disciples and the crowd witnessed God's miraculous provision. Not only was everyone satisfied, but there was an abundance of leftovers.[24]

The response of the crowd was that they wanted to make Jesus king right then and there. Knowing it was not His time, or God's design, He slipped away.[25] Jesus frequently went away to pray and find rest.

The next day, when the crowds realized Jesus had left the area, they got into boats and went to Capernaum to find him. When they found Him, His response was one that set them back. He said, "Very truly I tell you, you are looking for me, not because you saw the signs I performed but because you ate the loaves and had your fill."[26] What an indictment! Jesus said they were seeking Him not because of who He is, but because their own needs were met. He went on to tell them they needed to seek food that doesn't spoil, but food that leads to eternal life. Jesus said the Son of Man would give them this food.[27]

The crowd asked Jesus what sign He would give to show He is who He said He is. They brought up the fact that Moses gave their ancestors manna in the wilderness, but Jesus replied that it wasn't Moses, but God who provided the manna. God the Father gave them bread that comes down from heaven and gives life to the world.[28]   The Manna Israel received when Moses led them was not given to them by Moses, but by God. Today, in front of them, stood a different type of Bread – Bread from heaven – but Bread just the same. Their response to His teaching is very telling of where they were in life.

Jesus spoke of being the Bread of Life, come down from heaven. The crowd was obviously on a different wavelength than Jesus. The crowd began to argue among themselves about how He could be living Bread from heaven since they knew He was from Galilee.[29]

Jesus said some things that were hard to understand here. As New Testament believers, with the benefit of hindsight, we can understand what Jesus was saying. As a first century Jew, it was difficult to relate to what Jesus was saying because of the religious system of their culture. However, everything Jesus was teaching was

10

portrayed in the feasts God had implemented in the Law. Because of the difficulty in understanding his teaching, many of those who were following him left and went home.[30]

It is clear there was a disconnect between what Jesus was talking about and what the people understood. Even His closest twelve disciples were perplexed. When Jesus asked them if they would leave him too, Peter replied, "Lord, to whom shall we go? You have the words of eternal life. We have come to believe and to know that You are the Holy One of God."[31] We have a choice of response when God says things we do not understand, which He inevitably will. We can choose to throw our hands up in exasperation and leave, or we can seek to understand. The disciples had left everything to follow Jesus and chose to stay and seek to understand. Others in the crowd did not want to work that hard and chose to leave and go home.

What was it that caused so many of Jesus' followers to leave Him? Why could they not grasp what He was trying to say? Was there a connection between Jesus' observation that the crowds were following Him just because He fed them and their willingness to leave Him so quickly?

We can see that many in the crowds were following Jesus because He met their physical needs. He fed them, healed them and gave them a sense of security to the point they wanted to make him King. When he exposed the shallowness of their convictions and explained who he really is, they left him. What is the reason behind their reaction? We might say that they wanted an easy road, but there is more to it than that. I wanted to discover the reason behind the explanation. Wouldn't you?

Jesus Heals a Demon Possessed Boy - Mark 9:1 - 19; Luke 9:28 - 43

Mark chapter 9 begins with a dramatic statement from Jesus, "Truly I tell you, some who are standing here will not taste death before they see that the Kingdom of God has come with power."[32] We know all those to whom Jesus was speaking have long since passed away. Mark put this statement at this point in his narrative because he is about to illustrate what Jesus stated in the first verse of the chapter. Mark illustrates this truth with two events.

The first event Mark describes is referred to as "The Transfiguration." Jesus took Peter, James and John with Him to the top of a local mountain. Luke 9:28 says they went there to pray. During the Transfiguration, Jesus' appearance changed. Luke records, "As He was praying, the appearance of his face changed and his clothes became as bright as a flash of lightning."[33] Mark simply says that, "His clothes became dazzling white, whiter than anyone in the world could bleach them."[34] Moses and Elijah appeared and spoke with Jesus about His soon departure back to Heaven.[35]

Peter, being the enthusiastic disciple, wanted to erect three tabernacles for Jesus, Moses and Elijah. Suddenly, a cloud enveloped them and a voice spoke from the cloud, "This is my Son, whom I love (Luke says, 'whom I have chosen'). Listen to him!" As quickly as it came, the cloud vanished and Moses and Elijah vanished with it. Jesus stood alone with Peter, James and John.[36]

Jesus desired to leave witnesses here on Earth when He went back to heaven to rejoin his Father. For those witnesses to be effective in spreading the message of who Jesus is, they had to see things others would not see. These three disciples were privileged to see the embodiment of the fulfillment of all God's promises. Here before them was Messiah! The Hope of Israel! The presence of Moses and Elijah gave Jesus the validation of both the Law and the Prophets of the Old Testament. Clearly, God was speaking to these men in ways no other humans have ever heard or seen. The Kingdom of God was present with power and the King had arrived.

The second event Mark shares with us to illustrate that the Kingdom had come with power was developing while Jesus, Peter, James and John were on the mountain. The rest of the disciples, who were near Caesarea Philippi were experiencing a challenge. A man brought his son, who was demon possessed, to be healed. The disciples were unable to cast out the demon and heal the boy. These were the same disciples who had already been sent out to heal the sick and cast out demons.[37] Not only did this attract a crowd, but the teachers of the law were there, arguing with the disciples.[38] The disciples had done this before, yet they could not cast out this demon and heal this boy. Why?

When the crowds saw Jesus return, "They were overwhelmed with wonder and ran to greet him."[39] Were they simply excited because they believed He could do something to intervene in this situation, or was there something about Jesus' appearance that caused the crowd to react this way? Exodus 34:29 - 35 reveals that, when Moses came down from being in God's presence for forty days and nights, his face was radiant. He covered his face with a veil because the people could not look upon him. Such was the residual effect on Moses' appearance, the people "were afraid to come near him."

From the way Luke phrases his statement, Jesus may well have projected a residual radiance from being transfigured on the mountain, just as Moses did centuries before. Yes, many people were generally drawn to Jesus because of who He is, but the phrase, "overwhelmed with wonder" indicates Jesus appeared different on this sighting. On this day, the crowds saw something unusually unique in His appearance.

Jesus saw the crowds, the teachers of the law and the argument that was going on with His disciples. "What are you arguing with them about?" Jesus asked. A man in the crowd explained what had been going on – how the disciples could not cast out the demon and heal the boy.[40]

Jesus was annoyed with His disciples for not being able to handle this situation. Jesus expected His disciples to have the faith to cast out the demon and heal the boy. When they could not do it, He rebuked them for their lack of faith.

In other instances, Jesus told the person who was healed, or saved, that their faith as the recipient had brought about the miracle. Here, Jesus disciplined his disciples as those who were to exercise power on His behalf for not having the faith. There is faith needed on the part of both the recipient and the vessel of God's power. The father of the boy demonstrated his faith by bringing the boy to Jesus through the disciples, but the disciples failed to bring adequate faith to the situation.

In a dramatic scene, Jesus confronted the demon and healed the boy. What the disciples could not accomplish, Jesus did with the authority of His command. After Jesus healed the boy and the disciples were alone with Jesus, they asked Him why they could not cast out this demon. Jesus replied, "This kind can come out only by prayer." Some manuscripts add "and fasting".

Questions: What about this situation was so different that the disciples could not cast out the demon? What about prayer and fasting makes it more possible to cast out demons? What was missing in the disciples' lives that prayer and fasting would strengthen? Are there some victories in the spirit that require the application of spiritual disciplines to become real in our lives? What about prayer in Jesus' life made it possible for Him to cast out this demon, while the disciples could not? Remember, Jesus laid aside his divine prerogatives and lived life in a human body as any other human being.[41] Jesus lived this life relying on the Holy Spirit so He could model for us how we are to live, relying upon the Holy Spirit.

We leave this chapter with questions. How could people in these stories see the miracles Jesus performed, hear Jesus' words and still not believe Him when He told them who he is? How could the Jewish religious leaders and teachers of the Law, who were supposed to be the most connected to God in their society, hear Him, see Him and still seek to put Him to death? Was it purely for jealousy, or was there more to it than that?

As relates to those disciples who did not understand what Jesus was saying about being the Bread of Life, Jesus said they were following Him to gratify their own needs. They were not following Him because they believed He is Messiah. Jesus spoke a lot in this section about being the true Manna from heaven. He also said we need to eat His flesh and drink his blood to have life. What does all this mean? It obviously was not literal in a physical sense, so what was it all about? What about Jesus' words caused so many people to stop following Him?

16

These same disciples who could not cast out the demon, had cast out demons previously. In Mark 6:7 and 12, we are told that Jesus sent out the Twelve and they cast out demons. However, they were not able to cast this one out. What about this situation was different that made it so they could not cast it out and heal the boy? Jesus said this kind cannot go out but through prayer. What about prayer would make it possible for them to cast it out?

As you read these questions, you likely had answers come to your mind. I know I did. But as I thought about those answers, I realized they were insufficient to fully explain what was behind the actions the people in these stories chose. There is something deeper lurking in the shadows of human awareness that moved the people in these stories to respond to Jesus as they did.

There is an answer behind all these questions. The journey to understand the answer begins with understanding how we as human beings are put together. Because of how we are made, we live life in two very distinct realms. We begin to explore that thought in the next chapter.

CHAPTER 2
Our Human Make-up

☙

*Then God said, "Let Us make man in
Our image, according to Our
likeness, ... So God created man in
His own image; in the image of God
He created him; male and female He
created them." (Genesis 1:26-27
NKJV)*

*"And the Lord God formed man of
the dust of the ground and breathed
into his nostrils the breath of life; and
man became a living soul (Genesis
2:7 KJV).*

*"And the Lord God caused a deep
sleep to fall on Adam and he slept;
and He took one of his ribs and
closed up the flesh in its place. Then
the rib which the Lord God had
taken from man He made into a
woman and He brought her to the
man" Genesis 2:21-22 NKJV.*

CHAPTER ONE WAS ALL ABOUT questions. The three
situations in the life of Jesus discussed in chapter
one are representative of the kinds of situations in
the Bible that sparked a lot of my questions. Our
minds may mull over questions like those asked in
chapter one and come up with answers that satisfy
our quest for a while. But for me, after some time
and study, there remained a nagging question

those superficial answers left unresolved. I needed to look deeper. There was something Jesus expected of people that went beyond such a surface and casual answer. I wanted to understand the 'why' behind the acts; the motivation behind the choices.

Here, in chapter two, I am going to share the beginning of my journey of discovery. It is the beginning of a journey to discover the 'why' behind the 'what'. As with any investigation, it is best to start at the beginning. My search led me to look first at the creation of the first man and the first woman as recorded in Genesis. The deepest root of the answer to all the questions in chapter one can be found here.

Genesis 1:27 tells us, "So God created man in His own image; in the image of God He created him; male and female He created them." For me, the key was to understand what the phrase, "In his image," means. Both male and female are created in God's image. In fact, many believe that only together do male and female provide a complete picture of the image of God as revealed in humanity.

There are numerous ways to discuss how we are created in God's image. In my quest for answers, my focus was on the relational aspect of our being. Before we talk about that, let's look at the three main lines of thought related to the makeup of a human being.

The first view of the nature of a human being is that we are an indivisible whole that cannot be dissected into distinctive parts. This holistic view of human beings involves noting that every human activity involves us socially, spiritually and physically. Anything in life that impacts one aspect of our lives, affects all areas of our lives.

The second view is that of dichotomy. In the early church, this view largely grew out of Greek philosophy and states that human beings consist of an inner, immaterial part, or soul and an outer, physical body. The heresy of Gnosticism in the first and second century grew out of this philosophy. Dichotomy addresses the existence of a physical as well as an immaterial world and has been thoroughly Christianized. The idea of the dualistic nature of humanity has been around for longer than the Greek philosophers and many Jewish and Christian scholars believe we are two-part beings. Dichotomy satisfies the idea of the existence of a spirit world as well as a physical world.

While many Christians favor the dichotomist view, it does not provide an adequate model for the reality of life. The dichotomist view fails to address either the idea that the Lord our God is One God, or the idea that God is One God revealed in three Persons. There is no natural correlation to the image of God in this view. There are predominantly two ways to see God in biblical literature. He is either seen as one, indivisible Lord, or he is one Lord revealed in three Persons as is apparent from a study of all scripture.

The third view of the makeup of a human being is that of trichotomy. The trichotomist view flows out of the idea that God is an indivisible whole revealed to humanity in three Persons – known in theology as the Trinity.[1] Carrying that view of God to the design of human beings, we see that we have a spirit, a body and a soul.

This view can be illustrated by thinking of an egg. Looking at an egg from the outside, it appears to be an oval, seemingly solid object that is a unified whole. Looking inside the egg, there is a clear material surrounding a yolk. Both the yoke and white are contained within a shell. This unified whole is a tri-part object.

Each part of the egg has a specific function to complete the purpose for which an egg exists, which is procreation. The shell protects the yolk and white. The egg white is a liquid medium in which the embryo develops and provides protein the chick needs to develop properly. The yolk is the source of food for the developing chick and contains all the fat in the egg.

If any of the three components of the egg are taken away, the possibility of the egg fulfilling its reproductive purpose in life is eliminated. Once fertilized, the egg is a unique whole that will produce new life if left to its natural course. An egg is an integrated whole whose reproductive purpose in life can only be fulfilled if it remains whole. However, the egg consists of three major, distinct parts.

In the same way, the case can be made from scripture that a human being is comprised of three, distinct components, but is an integrated whole that must remain whole if the person is to fulfill their purpose in life. We are a living soul, that lives in a physical body and we have within us a spirit, that is the spark of life. This view is known as the trichotomist view of humanity. The trichotomist view is distinctly Christian and flows from the doctrine of the Trinity. This view fully captures the idea of human beings created in God's image, for we see God revealed as Father, Son and Holy Spirit. However, there is no indication that any Person of the Trinity correlates to a specific aspect of humanity.

The diagram below is a common diagram used in Christian thought to illustrate the triune nature of a human being. There are many variations of this diagram used today, but they share the common theme of three, concentric circles with spirit in the center and body in the outer ring.

Spirit is in the center because it is at the center of our being that we live from the spirit. In John 5:38, Jesus said that "Rivers of living water will flow from within them." It is this idea of the spirit being the deepest part of our being that places the spirit in the center of this diagram. Body is the outer circle because our bodies are the outward representation of the internal person. Soul is in the middle because it is influenced by both the body and the spirit.

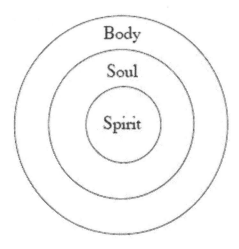

Genesis 2:7 says, "And the Lord God formed man of the dust of the ground and breathed into his nostrils the breath of life; and man became a living soul (KJV). This verse relates how God formed the first man from the dust of the Earth, then breathed into him. In verses 21-22 of the same chapter, we read," And the Lord God caused a deep sleep to fall on Adam and he slept; and He took one of his ribs and closed up the flesh in its place. Then the rib which the Lord God had taken from man He made into a woman and He brought her to the man." (NJKV)

We are not specifically told how God created the woman as we were with the man in verse seven. It is a natural and reasonable assumption that God breathed into the woman he formed and she too became a living soul. Except for the physical material, God used to create them, the creation process was the same for both the man and the woman. God formed the body, then breathed into them and they became living souls.

The Human Body

That we have a physical body is indisputable. The fact that we see, hear, smell, taste and feel the physical world around us establishes that fact for us every day. Our bodies were designed and fashioned by the hand of our Creator to enjoy the physical world and to feed inputs from that world to our inner being. We not only receive input from the world around us, we also project inputs to other beings in our world. We give and receive communication of all kinds through our bodies. Through our bodies, we enjoy all the beauty and goodness in the physical world. We also experience relationship with other people and animals in the physical world. Our bodies are only capable of receiving inputs through the five senses above. There are other stimuli we project and receive as human beings as well, but those are not physical in nature. They belong to a different dimension.

The physical body seeks its own comfort and satisfaction. The body constantly sends impulses regarding its needs and desires to the brain. Whether it is warmth when cold, cool when hot, food when hungry, gratification when desirous, or relief from pain; the body seeks its own comfort. Desire, instinct, impulse and reflex are key movers of our actions in the physical realm. Through these physical impulses, the body is constantly

24

attempting to influence our choices to maintain a level of comfort and satisfaction for itself.

The physical body is also one of the avenues available to us to communicate with other human beings. We were designed for relationship with each other. If we were limited to only receiving inputs, we would not be capable of relationship. We have the capacity of speech and touch and can make motions so others can see us. These avenues of interaction make relationship with other human beings possible.

Chapter two of Genesis ends with this from verse 25, "Adam and his wife were both naked and they felt no shame." Feeling shame, or the lack thereof, is an experience beyond the physical realm. That Adam and Eve were naked and felt no shame indicates their relationship was deeper than any of us can comprehend. It was a relationship that was beyond the physical nature. The relationship included another dimension.

The Human Spirit

With Creation complete, the first man and the first woman were together in the Garden. They were not alone, but the One who was there with them was more than physical. When God created them, he created them with another capacity. They were created with a capacity that allowed them to have a relationship with God, who is Spirit. That same capacity also added a dimension to their relationship with each other.

All through scripture, we are told that God is spirit: from Genesis, "...and the Spirit of God was hovering over the waters"[2] to Revelation, "Whoever has ears, let him hear what the Spirit says to the churches,"[3] it is clear from scripture that God is of a different dimension than our physical experience. Also, the idea of the Spirit, or of having a spiritual life, is not just a New Testament idea or experience.

The Spirit of God came upon the Old Testament characters such as Moses and the elders of Israel, "So Moses went out and told the people the words of the Lord and he gathered the seventy men of the elders of the people and placed them around the tabernacle. Then the Lord came down in the cloud and spoke to him and took of the Spirit that was upon him and placed the same upon the seventy elders; and it happened, when the Spirit rested upon them, that they prophesied, although they never did so again."[4]

The characters we read about in the Old Testament were enabled to do what they did because of the Spirit of the Lord. Gideon was a man who threshed wheat in secret because of the Midianite oppression, but when God's Spirit came upon him, he conquered thousands.[5]

Samuel was a man who was dedicated to God from birth by his mother.[6] There is an interesting exchange the first-time Samuel hears the Lord's voice. The story is told in 1 Samuel 3:1-21. Samuel was asleep when he heard a voice call his name. He lived with the High Priest, Eli and he thought Eli had called him. He went to Eli, but Eli said he had not called him. This happened three times before Eli realized that Samuel was hearing God call him. He instructed Samuel to reply, "Speak, for your servant is listening." As a result of heeding God's voice throughout his life, Samuel had a very powerful relationship with the Lord. He anointed the first two kings of Israel and led Israel in a transition from the period of the judges to the period of the kings.

The Spirit of God came upon Saul[7] and David[8] for it was by God's Spirit they were empowered to reign and accomplish progress for Israel. When the Spirit of God left Saul,[9] an evil spirit gained a foothold in his life. His life began to fall apart, and he was ultimately killed in battle. The mantel of kingship was taken away when the Spirit of the Lord left him.

Zechariah was a prophet during the time of the rebuilding the Temple in Jerusalem after the Babylonian exiles returned to Judea. The work was challenging, and the faith of the people wavered in the face of persecution and struggle. In Zechariah 4:6, we read, "Not by might nor by power, but by my Spirit, says the Lord Almighty." The temple was eventually completed by Zerubbabel.[10]

In the Gospel of John, Jesus told the Samaritan woman at the well that, "God is spirit and his worshippers must worship in the Spirit and in truth."[11] After He was risen, Jesus breathed on His disciples and said, "Receive the Holy Spirit."[12] Jesus also spoke of sending the "Spirit of truth" to His disciples after He was resurrected and back in heaven.[13]

We know that God is spirit. When God breathed into the man and woman during creation, He breathed into them spirit and they came to life. God, who is Spirit, breathed into physical material in the shape of the man and the woman and they became living souls.

The word for spirit in both the old and new testaments is the same root word that is used for wind, or breath. Though we may not be able to fully grasp the idea, there is something distinctly unphysical about our nature. It is a spark of spirit life that allows us to relate to God, who is Spirit. That spark also animates our physical bodies. When Jesus was crucified, He committed His spirit into the hands of the Father and His body died.[14] Stephen's death in Acts was similar in that he asked God to receive his spirit as he died.[15]

We were created with a spirit through which we can know God and understand His ways. It is the only capacity we have for fellowship with God because God is spirit. He designed us to have relationship with Him, so He made us spiritual beings, as well as physical beings. It is through this spiritual capacity that we can know God and the inner workings of our own humanity.[16]

In Genesis chapter two, Adam and Eve knew a fellowship with God we cannot begin to understand. They were innocent and pure. Their existence was untainted by sin and corruption. Not only were they able to have relationship in the physical realm, they enjoyed a spiritual relationship with their Creator and with each other. Paul wrote that we see through a mirror dimly when we look at spiritual life in Christ.[17] In our present state of human existence, we can only begin to experience the reality of God's presence. While there have been many who enjoy tremendous spiritual experiences, most of us only graze the surface of what we will experience when we leave the physical body and enter God's presence.

The Bible teaches us that there is a whole spiritual realm around us: angels, fallen angels and God. Our only capacity to connect to this realm and to discern what is going on in this realm, is through the spirit God created as part of our being. Just like our physical body is the vehicle through which we project and receive information from and to the physical world around us, our spirit is a communication vehicle through which we project and receive information to and from the spiritual world around us.

Most of us have been in a situation where we felt something just wasn't right. Or maybe we had an odd feeling about a person, and we find out later he or she was not a good person. Conversely, there are times we meet someone new, talk with them for a very short time and feel like we have known them our whole lives. These kinds of perceptions are from the human spirit. The ability to sense beyond the physical realm are spiritual capacities that are completely natural to our being.

As surely as we have physical DNA, we also have spiritual DNA. Our bodies all have certain common characteristics such as ears, eyes, hands and so on, but we each have a unique combination of shapes and sizes that make us uniquely us. The same is true of our spiritual nature. We are as unique in our spirits as we are in our bodies.

Our spirits are the source of deeply rooted motivations, creativity, faith, selfless love, goodness, discipline, joy, peace and compassion, among other traits. Spirit moves us to sacrifice on behalf of others. Our spirit is where the selflessness of our natures exists. God has put within each one of us specific spiritual abilities. Our spiritual capacities and talents can only come to full fruition through relationship with our Creator. Apart from relationship with Him, our spiritual capacities are corrupted and incapable of being fully expressed for their intended purposes.

Both aspects of our nature so far have been relational vehicles through which we relate to the physical and spiritual worlds around us. Each of those vehicles has unique characteristics of design, ability and natural skill or gifting. Neither the body, nor the spirit, are the total or real us. There is a third aspect to our nature that is the core of what is communicated through the vehicles of body and spirit.

The Human Soul

Our physical body is a medium through which we communicate and relate with the physical world around us, whereas our spirits are the medium through which we relate to the spiritual world around us. The soul is the "we" that does the relating through those two parts of our being. While body and spirit have unique characteristics, soul is the unique you. Soul is where we have the power of reason. Soul is the seat of emotion. The power of choice is also resident in the human soul.

Soul is where the action of life takes place. The soul is the seat of personality and the essence of our identity. The King James Bible presents Genesis 2:7 in a rich way, "And the LORD God formed man of the dust of the ground and breathed into his nostrils the breath of life; and man became a living soul." The soul is who we are. The body and the spirit are avenues through which who we are interacts with the physical and spiritual worlds around us. The soul is you. Your body can fail and die, but you (soul) still live. The spirit may be cut off from God, but you (soul) remain with the power to reason and to choose.

Soul is where the intangible and tangible aspects of our being intersect and combine. It is not always easy to distinguish between body, spirit and soul;

31

especially between soul and spirit. The fact is that because we are an integrated whole, it can be hard to consciously determine at times what part of our being is the origin of a specific impulse.

Soul takes inputs from both the physical and spiritual realms and attempts to make sense of them, to analyze them and to make decisions based upon those inputs. Soul contains emotion, so we can have an emotional reaction to any input. Our emotional response to stimuli often confuses our capacity to analyze inputs from either realm.

Soul is where responsibility for our actions lies, because it is in our souls, we make decisions about our beliefs and actions. Many things can influence our choices, but we always make the choice. Spiritual impulses, beings and forces attempt to move us one way or another, but we make the choices. Our bodies can send impulses that try to sway our power of choice, but we choose. Soul processes the input from the physical and spiritual worlds and makes decisions based on our ability to reason.

Emotions reside in the soul and play a role in many of our decisions. Emotions are often confused with motivators of the spirit. For example, the spiritual quality of joy, is different from the emotion of happiness. Emotions have been studied for centuries, so it is not possible to come up with one, universally accepted categorization of emotion. However, there seem to be six core emotions:

affection, happiness, surprise, anger, sadness and fear.

One way in which emotions impact our decisions is, if we like someone, we are likely to make choices that favor them. However, if we dislike someone, we are likely to make choices that do not favor them. We are less likely to make a quality decision if we are fearful, stressed, or experiencing surprise. Emotions tend to interfere with rational thought and need to be carefully considered when making important decisions.

Someone might ask, "Why is it important to identify the tri-part nature of our beings?" It is important for two reasons. First, understanding our tri-part nature is important because it is a significant aspect of human beings reflecting the image of God. God is a unified whole expressed to His creation as three Persons – Father Son and Holy Spirit. Like Him, we are a unified whole comprised of body, soul and spirit.

Understanding our tri-part nature is also important because it explains why we were created in the first place. The discussion above states that we have a body to have relationship with the physical world and people around us. We have a spirit to relate to God and his spiritual realm. Our purpose is heavily rooted in relationships, both with our Creator and with other human beings.

In the Ten Commandments, which is the center of the Mosaic Law, we see that the first four commandments relate to our relationship with

God. The last six commandments deal with our relationship with each other.

"And God spoke all these words:

² 'I am the LORD your God, who brought you out of Egypt, out of the land of slavery.

³ 'You shall have no other gods before me.

⁴ 'You shall not make for yourself an image in the form of anything in heaven above or on the earth beneath or in the waters below. ⁵ You shall not bow down to them or worship them; for I, the LORD your God, am a jealous God, punishing the children for the sin of the parents to the third and fourth generation of those who hate me, ⁶ but showing love to a thousand generations of those who love me and keep my commandments.

⁷ 'You shall not misuse the name of the LORD your God, for the LORD will not hold anyone guiltless who misuses his name.

⁸ 'Remember the Sabbath day by keeping it holy. ⁹ Six days you shall labor and do all your work, ¹⁰ but the seventh day is a Sabbath to the LORD your God. On it you shall not do any work, neither you, nor your son or daughter, nor your male or female servant, nor your animals, nor any foreigner residing in your towns.

¹¹ For in six days the LORD made the heavens and the earth, the sea and all that is in them, but he rested on the seventh day. Therefore, the LORD blessed the Sabbath day and made it holy.

¹² 'Honor your father and your mother, so that you may live long in the land the LORD your God is giving you.

¹³ 'You shall not murder.

¹⁴ 'You shall not commit adultery.

¹⁵ 'You shall not steal.

¹⁶ 'You shall not give false testimony against your neighbor.

¹⁷ 'You shall not covet your neighbor's house. You shall not covet your neighbor's wife, or his male or female servant, his ox or donkey, or anything that belongs to your neighbor'" (Exodus 20:1-17 NIV).

When Jesus was asked about the greatest commandment, His response was, "'Love the Lord your God with all your heart and with all your soul and with all your mind.' This is the first and greatest commandment. And the second is like it: 'Love your neighbor as yourself.' All the Law and the Prophets hang on these two commandments."[18] That sounds like relationship, doesn't it? The very core of our being is made for relationship with both our Creator and our fellow created beings.

In our current state, we do not experience either relationship with God, or relationship with other humans the way we were intended to experience them. When God completed creation, He looked at it and said, "It is very good."[19] We do not currently live in that perfectly completed world that God created. Something happened between that blissful moment of completed creation and our world today. We will look at what caused the change in the next chapter.

CHAPTER 3

Aftermath of One Choice

෬

*"So when the woman saw that the tree
was good for food, that it was pleasant
to the eyes and a tree desirable to
make one wise, she took of its fruit
and ate. She also gave to her husband
with her and he ate." Genesis 3:6
NKJV*

*"... by one man's disobedience many
were made sinners..." Romans 5:19
NKJV*

THE FIRST MAN, ADAM AND the first woman, Eve, were created with a spirit to have intimate relationship with their Creator. Genesis 3:8 tells us that God walked in the garden with Adam and Eve. After they ate of the Tree of the Knowledge of Good and Evil, they hid from God. From the previous verses, we understand this was not something they would normally do. We do not know how long it was between the time God created Adam and the time the couple were tempted. We do know that God walked with Adam in the Garden. Imagine, walking with God in an untainted, uninhibited, open relationship where the spiritual connection is as vibrant as the physical reality. Sadly, it is beyond our ability to comprehend the depth and intensity of what Adam and Eve experienced in God's presence before their disobedience.

God gave them everything in the Garden as food with one exclusion. God commanded them not to eat the fruit from one tree.[1] Adam apparently was alone when God gave him this command, but it is clear Eve understood the command because she repeated God's instruction to Satan during his temptation of her.[2] It is hard to imagine how anyone could have the relationships Adam and Eve enjoyed with God and each other and be seduced by the desire for more. After all, we simply have not and cannot experience life the way they experienced it. We have only known life after that ideal, human state was lost. Despite what they had, they were subject to desiring more. From the beginning, it is a universally exhibited trait of human nature to desire that which we do not have.

Sin appeals to all of us in ways that are revealed in this first temptation of humanity. Genesis 3:6-7 shows human weakness in action. There are four ways sin appealed to Adam and Eve. Sin continues to this day to entangle every human being in the same four ways.

The first enticement Eve encountered was that the fruit was good for food. She saw the fruit would satisfy her physical hunger. Our flesh desires satisfaction. From food, to warmth, to sexual fulfillment, our bodies constantly seek what is called a homeostatic level of comfort and satisfaction. Even before humanity's fall from their blissful existence, our first ancestors' physical bodies were designed to maintain comfort. Satisfying these basic biological needs is the first appeal of sin. This is called the desire, or lust, of the flesh and is strictly a physical enticement. None of these desires are wrong in and of themselves. In fact, God looked at the humans he made that were part of his creation and said, "It is very good."[3]

The desires of the flesh become sin when they move us to choose a direction away from relationship with God. Eve desired the fruit for food. It was not for lack of food that she desired it. It was that the fruit was something new and desirous she had not experienced. She perceived it to be satisfying and fulfilling to her body.

The second appeal of sin is revealed in the next phrase in verse 7, "pleasant to the eye." Sin often plays on our attraction to beautiful things. The pull is to possess them as our own. This is called the desire, or lust, of the eyes. It makes us feel good just looking at it. Looking at it moves us to desire to possess that which appeals to us. This appeal of sin comes to us in the form of the things we can desire that we long to possess. These desires can be for a car, or a job, or a certain income, or even an attractive partner. We desire that which catches our eye. The possession of beautiful things, or being around appealing people, also feeds into the next enticement.

The third appeal of sin is to our sense of ego, or pride. Eve saw that the fruit was desirable for gaining wisdom. Satan appealed to Eve's pride when he said, "when you eat from it your eyes will be opened and you will be like God."[4] This appeal is to the desire in all of us for significance, for power and influence. We all want to feel that we have value; that others look up to us and respect us. Eve saw that the fruit would give knowledge, that she could be like God. It appealed to her sense of wanting self-worth and value, so she took it and ate it. A distorted sense of pride is among the deadliest of things human beings can give in to.

The fourth appeal of sin is more relational, but just as powerful as the other three enticements. Verse 7 continues, "She also gave some to her husband who was with her." Notice that, Adam was with her. Eve's temptation did not happen in a vacuum. Her husband was with her. Why didn't he stop her? Why did he not rebut the words of Satan? Could it be that he too was duped? The apostle Paul writes that Eve was deceived, not Adam.[5] So, if Adam was not deceived, why did he eat the fruit? Adam did not want to lose his wife, so he went along. He did not want to be alone again. Adam had been given the love of his life; his perfect match. As he watched what was happening, he had to choose. In the end, he desired Eve's companionship and his relationship with her more than he desired relationship with God. In one decision, humanity was changed forever and paradise was lost to the human family.

God created the man and the woman as relational beings. He created them to have relationship first with Himself, but He also created them to have relationship with each other. The loss of relationship, especially an intimate relationship, is one of the deepest and most painful experiences we can face in life. Before we judge Adam too harshly, we need to put ourselves in his situation. Whether we like to admit it or not, if we were about to lose what Adam believed he would lose, we would make the same choice Adam made. Our sense of wanting to belong is simply that strong.

Adam chose to remain in relationship with Eve and in doing so, sacrificed the intimate relationship with God he had experienced since his creation. As with all choices we make, there are consequences to our actions. The first consequence of this choice was separation from the intimate relationship Adam and Eve had with God before they disobeyed. It was spiritual separation from God that resulted in death for the first man and first woman. The idea of death in scripture carries with it the idea of separation. Spiritual death is separation from God's presence. Adam and Eve's spirits did not cease to exist, but they experienced the death of being separated from the presence of God, who gives life. This is the first type of death Adam and Eve experienced.

The second type of death Adam and Eve experienced is the death of the physical body. Ecclesiastes 12:7 says, "then the dust will return to the earth as it was and the spirit will return to God who gave it." In both spiritual and physical death, the idea of separation is present. Ultimately, we will all experience this separation from our physical body. We will learn later that at least some human beings will be given a new physical body. Prior to the fall, Adam and Eve enjoyed a body that would not die.

A third type of death human beings will experience, though thankfully, not all will experience this death, is eternal death. Eternal death is eternal separation from God in a place of torment and suffering. Those who experience eternal death, will enter it once the current physical body dies. In Matthew 25:46, Jesus said some would go to eternal life while others would go to everlasting torment.

In addition to death, another consequence of their disobedience was that corruption entered the human family. Adam and Eve ate the fruit of the knowledge of good and evil. From that one choice, something happened inside them that went beyond merely making a bad decision. Consuming the fruit did something to Adam and Eve. Look at Genesis 3:7, "Then the eyes of both of them were opened and they realized they were naked, so they sewed fig leaves together and made coverings for themselves." The fruit they ate changed their perspective. The knowledge of good and evil outside an obedient relationship with God brought corruption to our race and Adam and Eve's offspring were forever infected.

Before Adam and Eve ate the fruit, they had a multidimensional relationship with each other.

They were as spiritually aware of each other as they were physically aware of one another. Their spirits were alive from daily walking in the presence of God. Their perceptions were uninhibited and untainted from the perception of good and evil. They had the capacity to know each other deeply, beyond a physical, mental and emotional knowing. Once they ate the fruit in disobedience, they became aware of their nakedness. They not only saw their physical nakedness, but they also saw their vulnerability to each other emotionally and spiritually. Physically, they covered themselves with leaves to hide from each other. They also began to hide from each other spiritually and emotionally. Human beings have been hiding from each other ever since. The fig leaves were an outward expression of changes happening in their hearts.

Genesis 3:9-10 reveals that not only did Adam and Eve hide from each other, they also hid from God. Corruption was already at work in Adam and Eve's lives. It is difficult for us in the twenty-first century to fully grasp what Adam and Eve lost, but we would do well to contemplate how their one choice impacted their posterity for all generations. With their one choice, the perfect egg of our triune human nature was broken with no immediate hope of repair.

Before we leave this chapter, I want to look at the third person who was deeply involved in Adam and Eve's disobedience. In traditional Jewish thought, the Serpent in Genesis chapter three is recognized as Lucifer, or Satan as he is referred to in the New Testament. Lucifer was an angelic being who at one time was one of God's main angels. He was swollen with pride and rebelled against God. Thinking he could take God's place, he took a third of the angels of heaven with him in his rebellion. The Bible only refers to him as Lucifer in his position before his pride filled fall.[6] He is a created being who is now called Satan.[7] When Adam and Eve were created, Satan was there to attempt to win them over to his side. He wanted then what he wants now. For all of humanity to follow him in his rebellion to the judgment he knows is waiting for him.

Look at Genesis 3:4. It reads, "'You will not certainly die,' the serpent said to the woman." This is in stark contrast to what God said to Adam in Genesis 2:17. Satan lied. In fact, Jesus said that Satan is the father of lies.[8] Satan is not our pal; he is not our friend. There is nothing good in him. He has no moral code that compels him to play fairly. He will lie, cheat, corrupt, steal, kill, destroy and deceive to accomplish his ends.

Satan deceived the first man and the first woman into disobeying God through lies and appealing to human vulnerabilities. He is working to do the same in our lives today. Satan has been deceiving humans for a long time and he is very good at subtly and persistently working to draw us away from our designed place in relationship with our Creator. He will use the culture around us and our own pride and insecurities against us. He will fabricate evidence and he will threaten us with ridicule and ostracization. He can appear as an angel of light,[9] meaning he can appear to be good, but his intent is always, not sometimes, but always malicious. He hates all of humanity. every individual. And he loves to corrupt our personal lives, our politics, our media and everything around us. His sole purpose is to deceive and decimate humanity as much as he can. In his twisted sense of reality, he is showing God that he, Satan, is superior. To him, human beings are nothing more than pawns to be used and abused for his perverse aggrandizement.

God's response to the disobedience of Adam and Eve is interesting. If God were an angry and vindictive God, he may have chosen to wipe the slate clean and start over. However, John tells us that, "God is love."[10] He created us for relationship. God still wanted relationship with Adam and Eve, only now there was something called sin in the way. God needed to deal with the divide sin created between Himself and His creation. We will look at how God chose to deal with His disobedient creatures in chapter five. But first, there is a story of how this corruption that impacts all of humanity impacted human society as history unfolded. Understanding how corruption has permeated our lives is crucial to finding the answers to our questions.

CHAPTER 4

A History of Corruption

ଔ

*"Then the Lord saw that the
wickedness of man was great in the
earth and that every intent of the
thoughts of his heart was only evil
continually." Genesis 6:5*

*But know this, that in the last days
perilous times will come: For men
will be lovers of themselves, lovers of
money, boasters, proud, blasphemers,
disobedient to parents, unthankful,
unholy, unloving, unforgiving,
slanderers, without self-control,
brutal, despisers of good, traitors,
headstrong, haughty, lovers of
pleasure rather than lovers of God,
having a form of godliness but
denying its power. 2 Timothy 3:1-5*

ONE MOMENT OF DECISION, ONE simple choice, by
the first man and the first woman resulted in a
great deal of personal loss for Adam and Eve. The
loss was not theirs alone, their decision to do what
God commanded them not to do brought pain and
suffering for all their posterity. The corruption that
began with the recognition of their nakedness
continued through the open door of their
disobedience to allow corruption to work in every
person and every generation of humanity.
Corruption's work was evident in the very first

46

generation of their children. When Abel brought a sacrifice that was pleasing to the Lord, Cain burned with jealousy because the sacrifice he brought was not pleasing to God. Cain had a choice. He could either learn from his error and discover how to better please God, or he could give in to the corruption that was working in his life and follow that path. Cain chose to follow the corruption and allowed jealousy and then hatred to move him to murder.

Chapters 4 - 8 of Genesis tell the story of the early expansion of humanity. Biblical history contrasts the line of Seth, Adam and Eve's third son, with the line of other human offspring. By Genesis chapter 7, God was fed up with his human creations and determined to wipe the slate clean and start over with Noah, a descendent of Seth and his family. From God's viewpoint, humanity had become utterly evil. Every person thought only evil all the time.[1] The flood wiped out every line of humanity, except Noah, his wife, his sons and their wives.

After the flood, God determined he would no longer curse the ground, nor would he destroy all living creatures as he had done in the flood.[2] He set the rainbow in the sky as a reminder of his promise.[3]

As humanity once again multiplied, corruption continued to work its way deeper into the human family. Eventually, God chose one man whose descendant would bring the culmination of God's plan to restore His human creations to Himself.

Abraham was the man God chose to be his witness to all peoples in all generations.[4] From his family line would be born, Jesus, the Messiah.

Abraham was a man who believed God. His faith toward God was such that God declared him righteous because of the faith he demonstrated.[5] God gave Abraham a promise that he would not only have a son, but that he would be the father of many nations. At the time of the promise, Abraham was old and his wife, Sarah was too old to have children. She had been barren all her life and now God was saying she would give birth to a son.[6]

Abraham and Sarah attempted to help God fulfill his promise of offspring for Abraham. Sarah insisted Abraham sleep with her slave girl, Hagar.[7] Modern Christians may baulk at this practice, but in the time and culture of Abraham and Sarah, it was common practice for a barren wife to give her servant to her husband to bear children for her. The result was that a son was born to Abraham. He was named Ishmael. Ishmael was not to be the son of promise. In fact, Abraham sent him away with his mother because of Sarah's jealousy and God's direction. God watched over Ishmael because he was Abraham's son and he too became a mighty nation.[8]

When Ishmael was about ten years old, Isaac was born to Abraham and Sarah. Isaac was the son God promised to Abraham, who was 100 years old when Isaac was born.[9] Even in that culture and time, Abraham was considered beyond the age of

48

being able to sire a child. Sarah was also beyond the normal age for giving birth to children. Isaac was the child of promise, while Ishmael was the son of human effort. Isn't it typical of us humans to think God needs our help in fulfilling His promises to us?

Isaac had twin sons named Esau and Jacob.[10] Esau was the older, but Jacob acquired the blessing that would normally go to the older son. Genesis 25:29-34 tells the story of how Esau despised his birthright and lost it to his brother Jacob. Esau was a hunter and came in from the open field about the time Jacob was making stew. The stew must have smelled very tasty, because Esau, feeling pains of extreme hunger, declared he was about to die. Jacob gave Esau some of the stew in exchange for his birthright.

The birthright was a lot more than an inheritance. It was passing down the family authority, the blessing from God that came down from Abraham. So, Esau despised this exalted place with God and gave it away to satisfy his physical hunger. Esau is another example of how we as human beings can neglect and even reject God's ideal for our lives. Esau, I am sure, was doing what he felt was important in the moment. What it cost him in the end is beyond measure.

Jacob became the offspring of Isaac that carried on the blessing of Abraham from God and the potential fulfillment of God's redemptive promise to Abraham. We hear about the God of Abraham,

Isaac and Jacob. Nowhere is Esau mentioned in that lineage. Jacob's twelve sons became the tribes of Israel. God changed Jacob's name from Jacob, which means deceiver, or manipulator, to Israel, which means prince. God's favor was on Israel, both the man and the nation.

As Jacob's family grew, jealousy developed between some of his sons. Jacob had children by four different wives. Two of his wives were sisters. The other two of his wives were the servants of the sisters. Rachel was the sister, whom Jacob loved most deeply, but like Sarah, she was not able to have children until she was much older. By the time she could conceive, Jacob was also older, but she bore him two sons. Joseph was the oldest son of Rachael and was one of Jacob's younger sons.

Joseph's brothers were jealous of him and sold him to Ishmaelite traders who sold him into slavery in Egypt.[11] At the time, Egypt was the most powerful nation in the world. Though Joseph was treated unfairly and imprisoned in Egypt, he served faithfully and eventually had the opportunity to interpret dreams for Pharaoh.[12] Through wisdom and intervention from God, Joseph warned Pharaoh of impending famine. He also gave Pharaoh a plan to provide for his nation and many people of the world. Joseph became the second most powerful man in Egypt and one of the most influential men of his time.[13]

When Jacob sent his remaining sons to Egypt to buy grain because of the famine, Joseph was in just the right position to save his family. In a deeply emotional reunion, Joseph revealed himself to his brothers. Joseph sent for Jacob, his sons and their families to come live in Egypt and enjoy the blessing of the land. Jacob moved his whole family to Egypt. There were sixty-six individuals that moved from Canaan to Egypt to join Joseph.[14] Little did any of them know at the time that their offspring would be in Egypt 400 years and become slaves which would fulfill the prophecy God spoke to Abraham about his descendents.[15]

Long after Jacob and Joseph died, there was a new line of Pharaohs in Egypt. They had neither any recollection about what Joseph had done, nor did they have any loyalty to his descendants. As a matter of expediency, the new Pharaohs enslaved Israel and put them to work as forced laborers.[16] Under this oppression, the family of Israel grew to be a nation of over a million people. Under the increasing oppression, Israel cried out to the God of Abraham, Isaac and Jacob. God heard their cry and called Moses to be his hand of deliverance for his people.[17] At the time of the exodus from Egypt, there were "about 600,000 men, besides children," Exodus 12:37. If we read "men" as adults, there were likely 1,500,000 people. If we read "men" as men of military age, there would have been about the same number of women and there would have been as many as 2,200,000 people.

Through Moses, God brought the nation out of bondage.[18] He gave them a system of laws and a pattern for worship. This was something totally new in the history of humanity. The Creator now called out one nation among all the nations upon which to place his name. Israel's assignment was to be a witness to the world. They were to be witnesses of God's desire to have relationship with the human beings He created in His own image.

God promised to give this generation of Israelites the land he had promised Abraham so many generations before.[19] Israel came to the edge of the land God promised and failed to enter by faith.[20] The generation that were slaves in Egypt all died in the wilderness. Only Kaleb and Joshua remained to lead the children of the slave generation into the promised land.[21] The people rejected God by not believing His promise of giving them the land.[22] By faith, obedience and hard work, the next generation conquered most of the nations of the land God had promised. Yet, even this faith filled generation of Abraham's offspring were not able to completely drive the nations out of the land.[23]

After Joshua, the leadership of the young nation died off and there was a long time when everyone did what was right in their own eyes. The period between the conquering of the promised land under the leadership of Joshua and the anointing of Saul as king is referred to as the period of the judges The Book of Judges records this period of Israel's history. A phrase repeated frequently in Judges is," There was no king in Israel. Everyone did what is right in their own eyes."[24]

The Book of Judges records all kinds of things that make us wonder about religious people. The reality is that religious people are no different than non-religious people. The people of Israel experienced a pattern repeatedly during the period of the judges. They would fall away from God. God would allow them to be conquered by a neighboring army. Israel would cry out to God. God would raise up a judge to deliver them. Israel would recommit their way to God, and they would be safe and secure until the next time they fell away from God.

When Israel sought God and made him the focus of their lives, everything went well. It was when they began to worship the idols of the nations around them and they forgot about the God of Abraham, Isaac and Jacob that they were plunged into bondage and despair. God continued to provide witness to Israel through deliverance and blessing because of his love for them and his promise to the Patriarchs.

After the period of judges, Israel reached a point that they wanted a king like all the nations around them.[25] God spoke through the prophet Samuel and said the nation was rejecting God as her king.[26] Nevertheless, God gave them a king. Saul was the first king Samuel anointed as the leader of God's people.[27]

Saul was a kingly king. By human standards, Saul looked like a king. He was head and shoulders taller than any other Jewish man of his time. He was from the tribe of Benjamin, who were known to be fierce warriors.[28] Saul was a man Israel could be proud to have as her king. God gave the nation what they wanted. They wanted a man to be king and rule over them and that is exactly what they got in Saul.

It wasn't long before things started going wrong with Saul. Saul was instructed to wait at Gilgal for Samuel to come offer sacrifices and bless the army before they fought the Philistines. Saul's men were getting scared and started to head for home. Because of his impatience, Saul offered the sacrifices only Samuel, as priest, had the authority to offer. As soon as Saul finished offering the sacrifice, Samuel arrived and rebuked him. Had Saul waited for Samuel, even if it had gone beyond the seven days, God would have established Saul's kingdom for all time. It was simply not Saul's place to usurp the role of priest. Because of Saul's presumption and failure to follow God's command, God rejected Saul as king and sought out a man who was more in tune with God's heart.[29]

God sent Samuel to anoint David, the youngest son of a Bethlehem shepherd to be the next king of Israel. God said that David was a man after his own heart. What was it about David that caused God to see him this way? It certainly was not that David was perfect. Scripture records David's adultery and conspiracy to commit murder.[30] We could ask – and should ask – what did God see in a man so flawed that He would call him a man after His own heart? One way to consider why God would say this about David is to compare him to his predecessor, Saul.

There were two things that Saul did in his life that show his heart. Both actions Saul took are recorded in 1 Samuel 15. Samuel was looking for Saul and he was told that "Saul has gone to Carmel. There, he has set up a monument in his own honor."[31] Earlier in chapter 15, Saul disobeyed the Lord in that God told him to destroy the Amalekites, to wipe them out and destroy all their possessions.[32] Saul spared the King and kept the best of the sheep and cattle, in direct conflict with God's command.[33] It was after this event that Saul set up a monument to himself. Saul's humble beginning as a young man who struggled with being made king had vanished. After only a short time of being king, he became enamored with self-importance.

The second thing Saul did that shows his heart occurred a little later in this same story. Samuel confronted Saul about his disobedience concerning the Amalekites.[34] In the end, God rebuked Saul for not obeying and took the kingdom from him. Had Saul been obedient to God, his kingdom would have been established forever. After Samuel told Saul the kingdom would be stripped from him,[35] Saul begged Samuel to honor him before the elders of Israel.[36] this shows that Saul was more concerned about his reputation in front of man than he was with his standing before God.

The first event shows us that Saul had become enamored with his own self-importance. The second event shows us that Saul sought the approval of man rather than the approval of God. Both characteristics of Saul moved him to disobey God.

In contrast to Saul's heart, David brought the Ark of the Covenant to Jerusalem and danced before the Lord as it was carried.[37] David also bought a place to build a temple to honor God as an offering to God. David could have had the property for nothing, but he said he would not offer to God that which was free.[38] David loved the Lord and desired to build a temple to replace the Tabernacle that had been the center of Israel's worship since the time of Moses. God would not allow David to build the temple because he was a man of blood.[39] David had been a man of war and bloodshed from his youth. His son, Solomon, would be a man of peace and more suited to building God's Temple.[40] David became king in a time of turmoil. It took a man of war to bring peace and security to the nation. God's anointing was on David for establishing the nation, not building the Temple.

David wrote 73 psalms that reveal his faith in many of life's situations. They show his heart for God and how he sought God's guidance, favor and approval. Saul became a man who sought his own honor, but David was a man who honored God. While David was far from perfect, his heart was oriented toward God. When he sinned, he repented and did not commit the same sin twice. God looks at our hearts. In David's heart, He saw a man who, though imperfect, sought God and put God's priorities for his life in first place.

Israel under David's leadership greatly expanded their borders. Under Solomon, David's son, Israel's political influence flourished. Solomon was given the task of building the temple his father David wanted to build. In addition to providing the place for the new temple, David provided many materials for building the temple such as gold, hewn stones for the walls and iron.[41]

Solomon made treaties with nations around them to bring in materials and craftsmen. Alliances were often consummated by marriage. Solomon allowed his many wives to bring in foreign idols. Eventually, it was his acceptance of these foreign gods that caused his zeal for the God of Israel to wane.[42] He also increased taxes on Israel to raise the funds to pay for the labor and materials. Solomon's reign was marked by relatively peaceful times militarily, but also major building projects and high taxes. By the time Solomon's son, Rehoboam became king, Israel was tired of the heavy burden the royal family had placed on them.[43]

While Solomon's life was one of luxury and excess, he is considered one of the wisest men who ever lived. The reason Solomon is seen this way is that, when God gave him a choice of what he desired most, Solomon asked for wisdom to lead God's people.[44] Solomon's wisdom was so admired that people throughout the known world would come to Jerusalem to hear his words.[45]

After Solomon died, Rehoboam, his son, became king. He was even harsher in his taxation and forced labor of the people of Israel than his father had been.[46] His defiance of the will of the people led to the dividing of the nation into two kingdoms. The Southern Kingdom consisted of the tribes of Judah and Benjamin, who remained loyal to the Davidic line of kings. The Northern Kingdom was made up of the rest of the tribes of Israel and had a variety of kings from different families.[47]

Jeroboam became king of the Northern Kingdom. He led the northern tribes away from God by setting up idols in the land. His sins were so egregious to God that throughout the history of the kings, he was used as a standard for the evil that kings did. Jeroboam set up an alternate form of worship in the Northern Kingdom that included golden calves and priests that were not from the tribe of Levi, as prescribed by the Law of Moses.[48] The Southern Kingdom was not much better. While there were several kings in Judah that lived in the ways of their father David, most of the Judean kings also followed in the sins of Jeroboam.

The nations that Israel deposed from Canaan were removed by God because of their wickedness. Israel was charged with not only defeating them, but they were to stay true to the worship of the God of Abraham, Isaac and Jacob and the Law of

Moses. Instead of living up to this divine directive, Israel followed in the ways of the peoples they conquered. In some cases, the idol worship conducted by Israel was worse than the practices of the nations they defeated.[49]

Over the course of hundreds of years, God sent prophets to both kingdoms to point out their sin and call them to repentance. As bad as their sin was at times, God always reserved for Himself a remnant of people who followed Him. Throughout the historical and prophetic books of the Jewish bible, God repeatedly showed Himself to be strong on Israel's behalf. This was especially true in the Southern Kingdom, where the line of David continued on the throne.

Eventually, God had enough and moved the Assyrians to defeat the Northern Kingdom in 722 BC. After a long subjection to Babylon, the Southern Kingdom fell, and Jerusalem was destroyed in 586 BC. The prophecy God spoke to Israel through Moses came to pass. In Deuteronomy 31:28-29, Moses said, "For I know that after my death you will become utterly corrupt and turn aside from the way which I have commanded you. And evil will befall you in the latter days, because you will do evil in the sight of the Lord, to provoke Him to anger through the work of your hands." Israel failed to maintain relationship with God. The corruption introduced to humanity through Adam and Eve infected not only Israel, but all the nations of the Earth. Israel had the law; they had the Tabernacle, then the

Temple. Israel had the prophets, the history, the traditions and kings. In the end, they repeatedly failed and fell away from the worship of Creator God. But there was always a remnant; a small band of people who would not forget God. As this core of believers spent 70 years in Babylonian captivity. God continued to speak to his people in exile through prophets like Daniel and Ezekiel. He continued to work in the lives of His devoted people.

God raised up a new king in Babylon, Cyrus, who was sympathetic to the plight of the Jews. He allowed the Jews to rebuild the walls of Jerusalem, then he allowed them to rebuild the Temple in Jerusalem. The books of Ezra, Nehemiah, Haggai and Zechariah tell much of this story. God used Cyrus to restore the Jews to their homeland, just as he had promised through the prophets. God never did restore the Jews of the Northern Kingdom, but for the sake of the promise he made to David, God restored Israel in Jerusalem.

Israel's struggles continued through what is called the Intertestamental period. This was a period of about 400 years between the return of Jews to Jerusalem from the Babylonian captivity and the birth of Jesus Christ when the New Testament books begin to record the history of God's interaction with humanity. During the time of Christ, the religious system of the Jews was greatly expanded. While the Law of Moses contained 613 commands, Judaism in the time of Christ consisted of thousands of rules. It was a religious system that oppressed the common people and kept those in positions of authority in power and privilege.

Looking over the history of Israel, several things stand out. First, in times that the nation turned to God, it was under strong leadership that followed God with sincere hearts and obedient actions. Sometimes that leadership was on a national level such as during the times of Moses, Joshua, David and Hezekiah. Other times, the leader God sent was to a local population such as during the time of the Judges and exemplified in the lives of Gideon and Deborah. Under strong leadership, Israel flourished. When strong, godly leadership was lacking, the nation experienced oppression from neighboring nations, an increase in idolatry, an active neglect of the purpose of the Lord and social decay.

The second thing that stands out is that the natural tendency of a society is downward, away from morality. This is the corruption that has entered humanity. It is not unlike the natural phenomenon of the Second Law of Thermodynamics which, simply stated, says that all natural systems degenerate when left to themselves.

A law is at work in each one of us that naturally subverts connecting with our Creator. Even those people whom God called righteous are seriously flawed. It is not on their own merits that God declares them righteous in His sight. We see the pattern in the earliest records in the book of Genesis all the way through the book of Revelation.

Corruption in the human family resulted in God's judgment of our predecessors with a great flood. After the flood, corruption again moved us away from relationship with God.

The corruption of sin in the human family extends beyond the individual. It permeates society and moves cultures away from God. It is a pattern often repeated in history that a nation, or people, will rally around a set of principles, or a strong leader, with the intent to be free from corruption and control of corrupt systems. The pattern continues until comfort sets into the society, often from having overcome the obstacle that caused them to unite in the first place. Then the corruption that is at work within the human family moves the society toward the same corruption it sought to escape generations before. Complacency breeds inattentiveness. Inattentiveness makes way for corruption to go to work. This is especially evident in Western cultures, in general and in the United States over the last 75 years.

A third thing that stands out is that as humans we tend to focus on structures and externals, but God calls us to a spiritual awareness. When we respond to His call, He can do things that defy natural laws and order. In the time of the Exodus and following, it was through seeking God and obeying Him that Israel conquered the nations living in the land God promised them. Seeking God and obeying Him are spiritually motivated actions that go against our natural propensities.

During the time of Judges, God raised up leaders to move either all or parts of the nation back to himself. These leaders sought God and were obedient to His call. They were responding out of a spiritual orientation.

As Samuel came on the scene to lead Israel as the last, national judge, Israel sought to be like the nations around them and asked for a king. They were not content with leadership that was wholly inspired by God. From a human point of view, it was too unpredictable. They chose not to be unique in that sense and they felt that having a king to rule over them would be better than to trust God. There was something in them that sought the external controls; the physical presence of a king to rule over them. Rather than lean on the Spirit guided life they experienced during the escape from Egypt, during the conquest of the land and during the period of the judges, they wanted a physical king they could look to. In asking for this, they rejected God's leadership.[50]

The fourth thing that stands out is people in power tend to like to exert that power over others and they will fight everything that threatens their power. God institutes leadership to serve the needs of the community and guide the individual. For example, God instituted the Law of Moses to point the way to relationship with Himself and our need for a sacrifice for our sins.[51] Attaining righteousness by observing the Law is simply not possible.[52] Humans perverted what God instituted and used it for personal gain and to exert control over the people. The priesthood under Eli became corrupt, using their positions to enrich themselves and serve their own pleasures.[53] The religious leadership during the time of Christ was utterly corrupt, using the religious system to advance their own comfort and exert control over the masses. The abuse of power over the powerless is one of the things that moved Jesus to directly assault the hypocrisy of the leaders of Israel.

If God had left humanity without hope in this state of corrupted nature, we would be a sorry bunch indeed. However, out of His deep love for each one of us, He devised a plan to deal with the corruption and sin in our lives and restore us to an intimate relationship with Himself. The next two chapters are devoted to outlining Creator God's plan to restore human beings to a right relationship with Himself.

CHAPTER 5
God's Plan to Redeem

ॐ

"⁸ But God demonstrates His own
love toward us, in that while we were
still sinners, Christ died for us. ⁹
Much more then, having now been
justified by His blood, we shall be
saved from wrath through Him. ¹⁰ For
if when we were enemies we were
reconciled to God through the death
of His Son, much more, having been
reconciled, we shall be saved by His
life. ¹¹ And not only that, but we also
rejoice in God through our Lord
Jesus Christ, through whom we have
now received the reconciliation."
Romans 5:8-11

'For "whoever calls on the name of
the LORD shall be saved."' Romans
10:13

In the last chapter, we discussed that death, as referred to by God in Genesis chapter two, has multiple aspects. The immediate result on the day our first ancestors ate the fruit that God forbade them to eat was that they lost their spiritual connection with God. They also experienced corruption in their beings that impacted their lives on multiple levels. Human beings lost intimate relationship with God. God, however, did not lose

His desire to have relationship with those He created. Their disobedience had consequences. One of those consequences is that they faced was God's justice. This principle is defined for God's economy in Deuteronomy 24:16, which says, "each will die for their own sin." Romans 6:23 says that the "wages of sin is death." God's justice demands that a price be paid for our disobedience. God is not only just, he does not have favorites, or show favoritism.[1] There are no backroom deals, no side arrangements in God's economy. Every human being is guilty.[2]

The idea that sin results in death is a universal, spiritual principle that governs God's creation for all times. Because God is holy, God's justice required a penalty for Adam and Eve's sin. Just as there are physical laws that govern our lives, there are also spiritual laws that govern our lives. The law of sin and death is one. The law of sowing and reaping is another. These are a few of the spiritual laws that impact our lives as much as the law of gravity impacts us. Though gravity impacts our lives in an observable way every day we rarely stop to think about it or how it impacts our lives.

Spiritual laws are the same way. Just as there are no bright, neon signs telling us daily that gravity keeps our feet to the ground, there are no signs reminding us of the impact of the spiritual laws on our lives. Our Creator God is a God of order. Our lives are supported and governed by both physical and spiritual laws whether we recognize them or not. The law of sin and death could have left us eternally separated from God and condemned to die. But, because God is also pure love, His love for His human creations would not allow His justice to destroy us. Out of love, God devised a plan to satisfy His justice and remove the barrier to relationship with His human creations.

All this may sound like God is schizophrenic, but He is not. He is holy, He is just, and He is love without conflict and without flaw. Where we see conflict between holiness, justice and love, God has a plan that was built on love, satisfies His justice and invites us to join Him in His holiness. God desires relationship with human beings, which He created in His own image. He created us with the freedom to choose to have relationship with Him or not. He wants us to use that power of choice to choose to have relationship with Him. If God wanted robotic worshipers, He would have created them. He desires to be in relationship with those who choose, of their own free will, to be in relationship with Him.

It is hard to comprehend the gravity of the consequences of Adam and Eve's choice to disobey God. Though it is challenging to understand, we fail to do so at our own peril. Their disobedience was a gross betrayal of an intimate relationship between God and His created treasure – human beings. The offense was great and if God was to make it possible for humans to have personal relationship with Him, then the cure would be just as dramatic as the offense. Scripture tells us a lot about how God set about to redeem humanity and make it possible for us to have intimate relationship with our Creator.

That first day of disobedience by Adam and Eve resulted in the first sacrifice for sin. Genesis 3:21 says that God made garments of skin for Adam and his wife. Animals died to provide a covering for Adam and Eve; blood was shed. Leviticus 17:11 says, "For the life of the creature is in the blood and I have given it to you to make atonement for yourselves on the alter; it is the blood that makes atonement for one's life." Further, Ezekiel says that the soul who sins is the one who must die. Each one of us is guilty before God.[3] The shedding of blood is a theme throughout scripture. It begins in Genesis and culminates at the cross where Jesus Christ was crucified. In our civilized culture, we may think that the shedding of blood is a brutal concept. The brutality of the sacrifice highlights the seriousness of our offenses before our Creator. He takes them very seriously and took great lengths, out of love for us, to make atonement for them.

Genesis 4:1-5 tells us about a time when Adam and Eve's first two sons brought offerings to God. Abel was a keeper of flocks and Cain tilled the ground. Both brought an offering to the Lord. Abel brought an animal from the firstborn of his flock. Cain brought a harvest from his fields as an offering to God. God looked favorably on Abel's offering, but Cain's offering did not get God's approval. Abel brought an offering containing blood, Cain did not. Had Cain purchased an animal to sacrifice and brought it with humility and an understanding heart, his offering would have been accepted.

God called Noah to build an ark in which to rescue humanity and the animals on the earth from the flood God would bring upon His creation. God brought the flood because of the complete corruption of humanity.[4] When the flood waters receded, Noah and all who were on the ark disembarked. Genesis 8:20 says that, "Noah built an altar to the Lord and took of every clean animal and of every clean bird and offered burnt offerings on the altar" (NKJV). The burnt offerings of Noah were a sweet aroma to the Lord. God was pleased with the offering and made three promises. God's response to the offering of blood with faith was one of promise, blessing and hope for humanity.[5]

In time, God chose Abraham and his descendants as his witnesses to the family of humanity. There were two distinct times in Abraham's life where animal sacrifices were intricately tied to his relationship with God. Genesis 15 details a time when God made a covenant with Abraham. God instructed him to bring a heifer, a goat, a ram (sheep), a turtledove and a pigeon for a sacrifice. Abraham split the animals in two, except for the birds and laid them before the Lord. A flaming torch came and passed between the pieces Abraham had laid out and the Lord made a covenant with him. The shedding of blood accompanied this life changing event in Abraham's life.

The second event in Abraham's life that is significant regarding a sacrifice is found in Genesis 22:1-19. In this chapter, God directed Abraham to sacrifice Isaac, his only son and the son through whom God's promise to him was to be fulfilled. Abraham's response reveals why his faith was credited to him as righteousness. In verses 7 - 8, Isaac asked his father where the lamb was for the sacrifice. Abraham's response was, "My son, God will provide for Himself the lamb for a burnt offering." Abraham's faith in God was such that he recognized that even if God required him to sacrifice Isaac, God would bring him back to life and fulfill His promise.[6] Abraham was obedient, even to the point of giving up his only son; the son through whom God promised to make Abraham a great nation. In the end, Abraham did not sacrifice Isaac, because God provided a ram for the sacrifice just as Abraham, by faith, had stated He would.[7]

Hundreds of years later, God himself provided the perfect sacrifice in His "only begotten Son". Abraham's experience looked forward to the day when God would give His Only Son as a sacrifice for all humanity.[8] There was no lamb to stand in the place of Jesus. Jesus is the Lamb that stood in our place.

Abraham's grandson, Jacob, also built alters and offered sacrifices to God. Genesis 35:1-15 relates a time when God called Jacob to go to

70

Bethel. Jacob had been to Bethel before when, as a young man, he was fleeing from his brother Esau. He stopped to rest at Bethel and God gave him a dream about his future and appeared to him there. The encounter gave Jacob hope at a time he wondered how, or even if, he would survive. The Genesis 35 event occurred 20 years later. God called Jacob back to Bethel to establish his home there. Verse 7 says that Jacob built an alter at Bethel and offered sacrifices on it. After Jacob offered his sacrifice, God renewed his covenant with him. He renamed him Israel and reaffirmed His promise to give Jacob's descendants the land of Canaan.[9] Once again the shedding of blood accompanied the renewal of a covenant promise between God and a human being.

In the days of Moses, the descendants of Jacob were slaves in Egypt.[10] The book of Exodus records God's deliverance of Israel from Egyptian bondage. God brought ten plagues on the Egyptian Pharaoh and his people. With each plague, Pharaoh continued to harden his heart and would not let Israel go free. In the final plague, God announced through Moses that the firstborn in all the land of Egypt would die. God saved Israel from this plague by initiating the Passover celebration.[11] Wherever Jews have lived since the Exodus, they have celebrated the Passover every year. Moses was told to instruct the Israelites that each family to set aside a one-year old ram that was spotless and perfect. They were to slaughter, cook and eat it in a specific manner. They were to take the blood of the lamb and brush it on the lintel and sides of the door frames. As the Angel of Death went through Egypt, every first-born human and animal died. It was the blood that was a sign for the Angel of Death to pass over the house. Everywhere else in Egypt, the first born of animals and humans died.

Of all the sacrifices in the Old Testament, the Passover sacrifice is one of the most significant. It is commemorated every year because God birthed a free nation at its inception. Israelites to this day are to look back on this event and remember what God did for the offspring of Abraham, Isaac and Jacob.[12]

When John the Baptist pointed to Jesus in John 1:29 and declared, "Behold! The Lamb of God, who takes away the sin of the world!", he was pointing to God's sacrificial Passover lamb. Jesus' sacrifice was to pay for the sins of all the world.[13] Both Peter and Paul refer to Christ as the Passover Lamb. In 1 Corinthians 5:7, Paul writes, " Get rid of the old yeast, so that you may be a new unleavened batch – as you really are. For Christ, our Passover lamb, has been sacrificed." Peter's reference is subtler when he writes, "For you know that it was not with perishable things such as silver or gold that you were redeemed from the empty way of life handed down to you from your ancestors, but with the precious blood of Christ, a lamb without blemish or defect" (1 Pet. 1:18-19). The Passover Lamb was to be a lamb without blemish or defect.[14] In the Hebrew mind, to whom Peter was writing, this was a clear reference to the Passover Lamb.

Just as God set Israel free from Egyptian bondage through the first Passover, He sets those free from bondage who come to Him with faith in what Jesus, the true Passover Lamb accomplished for us.

When God revealed His law to Moses, there were many requirements for animals to be sacrificed. Any time there was to be forgiveness for sins, or purification of an item, or consecration of the people, blood was shed. The blood was often sprinkled on objects, or people, who were being set apart, or sanctified for service. These sacrifices were required not because God delights in the slaughter of animals, but because he is consistently communicating to humanity that living apart from an obedient relationship to God has a high price. The price that must be paid is death, or the shedding of blood.[15] The rightful penalty for our sin is our personal death. God is telling us through the Passover and the sacrifices of the Law that there is to be a vicarious sacrifice that pays the penalty for all humanity. Jesus came to fulfill the law of sin and death on our behalf.[16]

The blood of animals was never enough to wipe out the penalty and corruption of sin. Nor was it ever intended to be enough.[17] The animal sacrifices in the Old Testament looked forward to God's perfect sacrifice in the future. Once Jesus offered His blood as a sacrifice for sin, there was no longer a need for animal sacrifices.[18] Jesus' blood fulfilled all the requirements because He was a lamb without spot or blemish, and he took the wrath of God's judgment for any who believe in Him. He died once, for all.[19]

God's redemptive plan involves two things. First, there had to be a death that pays the penalty for our disobedience. The blood of the sacrifices of the Law of Moses were not enough. Jesus is that sacrifice. He took on our sin and paid the penalty in full because he was the perfect sacrifice. He is the Lamb that took all God's wrath and justice upon himself.[20] So our Creator God took care of everything that could possibly separate us from His love and from a personal relationship with Him.[21]

The second thing required for God's plan to work for us is our acceptance by faith of His plan. In this plan, we acknowledge our sin and accept His forgiveness, which He purchased for us and gives us freely in Christ. God will not make our choices for us. He created us with free will, to choose relationship with Him, or to reject relationship with Him. We get to choose.[22]

Take a moment to consider God's offer this way. Imagine yourself at a large banquet table. The table is full of all kinds of food. All your favorites are on the table: roasted turkey, ham, fillet minion, mashed potatoes, fresh salad and fruit, steaming hot, fresh baked rolls. The aroma is tantalizing. The food is the best-looking food you have seen in ages. Not only is your stomach growling because it is after 1:00 and you had breakfast at 6:30 this morning, but you also hear the other people's stomachs growling. The food is there for the taking, you have been invited to sit and eat whatever you want. While it is inconceivable that anyone would do so, you could starve to death sitting at that table. If you never chose to reach out and take some food for yourself, you could sit there amid all that food and die from starvation. In the same way, Jesus set the banquet table for us to have relationship with God, but he won't force us to make the choice to take advantage of all He has provided. We must make that choice ourselves. No one can choose for us. We can choose for no one else. We can starve. Or, we can feast. The choice is ours and ours alone.

If you have never prayed to accept God's gift of forgiveness, now is a good time to ask God to forgive you and enter a new relationship with your Creator. God's gift is free, there is nothing to do to purchase it, or deserve it. All we need do is believe and receive. The following is an example of how to pray.

Dear God in heaven, I come to you in the name of Jesus. I admit to You that I have sinned. I am sorry for my sins and the life that I have lived; I need your forgiveness.

I believe that your Son, Jesus Christ, shed His precious blood on the cross and died for my sins. I am now willing to turn from my sin, accept Your forgiveness and learn to live in a way that pleases You.

You said in Romans 10:9 that if we confess that Jesus is Lord and believe in our hearts that God raised Jesus from the dead, we shall be saved.

Right now, I confess Jesus as the Lord of my life. With my heart, I believe that You raised Jesus from the dead. This very moment I accept Jesus Christ as my personal Savior and according to His Word, I am saved.

Thank You, Jesus, for Your willingness to die in my place which has saved me from God's wrath because of my sin. Thank you, Father God, for Your grace that gives me salvation. I understand that your grace and forgiveness does not give me license to go on sinning. Therefore, Lord Jesus transform my life so that I may bring glory and honor to you alone and not to myself. Thank you, Jesus, for giving me eternal life. AMEN.

Please understand. It is not the words we repeat that save us. It is the heart-felt belief in Christ and His work that saves us. Confessing that which is true in our hearts is the natural outflow of faith. If you just prayed that prayer, I encourage you to share your decision with someone. Perhaps a relative, or a friend, or a co-worker has shared something about the good news of Jesus with you in the past. Let them know of your decision and that you asked for God's forgiveness. They will be happy their prayers have been answered and will be able to help you find resources to help you grow in your relationship with your Creator.

Now what? Salvation is not a onetime experience. It is something we experience at a point in time. But, when we first come to Christ by faith, we begin a journey that will last a lifetime and through all eternity. The next chapter outlines the scope and depth of the journey that began for all of us with a prayer such as the one above.

CHAPTER 6
Restored in Three Phases

☙

"⁸ For by grace you have been saved through faith and that not of yourselves; it is the gift of God, ⁹ not of works, lest anyone should boast. ¹⁰ For we are His workmanship, created in Christ Jesus for good works, which God prepared beforehand that we should walk in them." Eph. 2:8-10

"¹² Therefore, my beloved, as you have always obeyed, not as in my presence only, but now much more in my absence, work out your own salvation with fear and trembling; ¹³ for it is God who works in you both to will and to do for His good pleasure." Philippians 2:12-13

"⁵¹ Behold, I tell you a mystery: We shall not all sleep, but we shall all be changed— ⁵² in a moment, in the twinkling of an eye, at the last trumpet. For the trumpet will sound and the dead will be raised incorruptible and we shall be changed. ⁵³ For this corruptible must put on incorruption and this mortal must put on immortality. ⁵⁴ So when this corruptible has put on incorruption and this mortal has put on immortality, then shall be brought to pass the saying that is written:

78

*"Death is swallowed up in victory." 1
Cor. 15:51-54*

There are three aspects, or phases of the
salvation Jesus purchased for those who accept His
gift of forgiveness and restoration. When we are
first saved, we are reborn spiritually. Our spiritual
capacity to have relationship with God is
awakened because the Holy Spirit, God's Spirit,
comes to live inside us. Through His in-dwelling
Spirit, our spirit is made alive to God.

When we were born physically as babies,
we started life separated from God spiritually. At
some point, as we grew from infancy to maturity,
we became accountable for our own decisions.
Many have questions about what happens to
children who die before the age of accountability.
The sacrifice of Jesus certainly is powerful enough
to have cleared the way for God to forgive such
infants. In Exodus 33:19, God tells us, "I will have
mercy on whom I will have mercy and compassion
on whom I have compassion." Ultimately, it comes
down to trusting that our Creator loves each
individual and desires relationship with all His
created beings. Remember, God is love and, in His
love, He has done and continues to do many things
that boggle our puny minds. We need to trust in
His love, not presume every decision He makes is
out of wrath.

Through faith in Christ, we are made alive to God
in Christ. We immediately have the capacity for an
intimate, spiritual connection with God that allows
us to begin to grow in our relationship with our

Creator because we have accepted His provision for our sin. Our human spirit is now in fellowship with the Spirit of God.[1] Like any relationship, it will be made stronger through attention, time together and commitment.

This is the initial phase of salvation and is called positional justification. Scripture says that we are seated with Christ at the right hand of God.[2] We are in Christ.[3] Spiritually we are with Him and He is with us. There is nothing we can do to become more saved than we are in the moment we first place our faith and trust in Christ. Our salvation is secured by His sacrifice and sealed with the Holy Spirit who now lives inside us.[4]

The initial phase of salvation is exciting because it is fresh and new. People frequently feel euphoric because, for the first time in their life, they are free from the guilt and burden of sin. They feel like a weight has been lifted off them. The initial sense of God's presence can be intoxicatingly refreshing. The new sense of peace we feel in His presence can make us feel like life will radically change overnight. We can experience high expectations for dramatic change in our circumstances and lives. In this initial phase of salvation, it is especially easy to base our faith on our feelings. Sometimes our circumstances do radically change overnight once we come to Christ. The Apostle Paul certainly had that experience. You can read about his experience in Acts 9:1-30. Often, however, instead of seeing our circumstances change quickly, we are given grace to endure and enjoy a new sense of hope, joy and promise while God moves in our hearts, lives and circumstances. God is at work in our lives because He loves us, so we need to stand with hope and faith even when physical circumstances do not change for us right away. In fact, many times circumstances and relationships become more strained when we first come to Christ. There are many reasons for this phenomenon, but we will look at that a bit more in chapter eight.

Our relationship with God established through our faith and provided by God's grace is like any other relationship. This initial phase of salvation establishes our position in Christ. Frequently, remembering the moment of salvation reminds us of the genuineness of our transformation. It takes effort on our part to nurture and develop this new relationship. The more we work at knowing God, the more we reap the benefits of knowing Him. A considerable challenge we face as we come to faith in Christ is that we are deeply conditioned by our culture and the physical world to be insensitive to the spiritual realities around us.

Moving beyond initial faith in Christ leads us to the second phase of our salvation, which is called sanctification. The Apostle Paul referred to this phase as the working out of our salvation with fear and trembling.[5] In this phase of our salvation we grow in our knowledge of God and our experience with God. We come to understand how God uniquely made us as an individual. We discover the works God has set apart for us to complete in this life.[6] The sanctification phase of being a Christian is challenging and will last the rest of our earthly lives. It is so challenging that many people fall away from the faith due to disappointment from unrealistic expectations. Many Christians fail to understand the battle they enter when they come to faith in Christ.

Jesus spoke of four heart conditions in Mark 4:3-8. These heart conditions represent the "soil" into which the seed of the Gospel is sown. He used a parable of seed being sown because He was speaking to a largely agrarian culture; the people He was speaking to understood about planting and growing seeds.

The first batch of seed was sown by the wayside. Wayside soil is ground that was unprepared for seed. The seed was quickly snatched away by birds. Jesus' explanation of this is that the birds are representative of Satan, who comes to snatch away the seed of the Gospel in human hearts.[7]

The second type of soil was stony ground. When the sun came up, the seed in this soil became scorched and died, because it could not take root and thrive. Jesus explained to His disciples that these are people who have no depth in their hearts; when trouble, or persecution come up, they stumble and fall away.[8] They are people who initially experience joy when they first believe, but because the seed does not take root, the heat of persecution or trial destroys their faith.

The third type of soil is full of thorns. The seed sown here started to grow, but it was choked out by the weeds that grew up around it. The good seed eventually died from lack of nutrition. It did not produce a harvest. This heart condition is a heart filled with the cares of this world, the desire for wealth and things other than God stop the seed from growing and it becomes fruitless.[9] These are the distractions and worries of this life. They are numerous and can subtly choke the life out of our faith.

The fourth type of heart soil is good ground. The seed sown on this soil took root and produced a bountiful harvest. It is not the quantity of harvest that is important, but the fact that the soil produced a harvest. Jesus said some produced thirty-fold, some sixty and other soil, an hundred.[10] This parable reminds us that we need to examine our own hearts. It is likely that most of us have a combination of soil in our hearts. The challenge we face is to continually be open to the work of sanctification the Holy Spirit wants to work in us, from the inside out, so that our hearts can be fertile soil for the Gospel to do its work. No heart soil condition is beyond the reach of the Holy Spirit to change it to fertile soul. We will look more at how we can partner with God's Spirit in this work in chapter ten.

In 2 Timothy 4:7, Paul said that he had run his race, fought the fight and kept the faith. Clearly, this is language that indicates struggle and the output of effort. The second phase of our salvation involves a struggle that will last our whole life. It is not a sprint, it is a marathon that takes effort, discipline and intentional effort. We do not like to hear that in the twenty-first century Western culture, but if we desire to follow Christ, we must get used to the idea that God uses a crock pot on our lives, not a microwave. Sometimes, all we can do is stand on our faith as the flood waters of life surround us. But if we persevere, we will see God turn our trials and struggles into meaningful growth and fruitfulness.

The third and final phase of our salvation is when our physical body dies, and we go to be present with the Lord. Sin is finally condemned in this earthly vessel. We get to exchange this body that is corruptible with one that is incorruptible.[11] In chapter four, we discussed how corruption has permeated all of humanity. When our physical body dies, we will leave that corruption behind and take on a new body that is free from sin and the impact of Adam and Eve's fall. Our personal redemption will be complete. In our new body, we will enjoy unhindered relationship with God and with our fellow human beings. The veil of human corruption and sin will be gone forever. We will know as we are known.[12]

Consider the body of Jesus after His resurrection. In His resurrected body, we see the model of our new bodies. In Luke 24:13-32, doctor Luke tells of two of Jesus' disciples walking from Jerusalem to a town called Emmaus. During this journey, they were joined by a third man who conversed with them. As they got close to the town of Emmaus, they invited the man to have dinner with them. Verse 31 says, "Their eyes were opened and they knew Him; and He vanished from their sight." Jesus' resurrected body was not bound by the physical laws of nature. He could appear and disappear at will.

In the Gospel of John, chapter 21 verses 19-29, John tells of a time after Jesus rose from the dead. The disciples were all together and Jesus appeared in their midst. He told them to feel the nail holes in His hands and put their hands in His side to confirm it was really Him. His was a body they could touch and see and hear. The wounds in His hands and side serve as an eternal reminder of the price He paid to restore us to relationship with our Creator. Paul taught that Jesus is the first fruits of those who rise from the dead.[13] We will have a body like His when we lay this present body down. The third phase of salvation is what we long for at the end of this life. It is a future hope that we have as believers in the sacrifice and resurrection of Jesus Christ. This final phase is the completion of God's plan to restore the whole egg of humanity, as we discussed in chapter two.

The newness of faith in Christ eventually wears off. We find ourselves in relationship with God, but often it is different than we first expected.

We find ourselves in the middle of the second phase of salvation. Living a faithful life in Christ can be challenging. There are many things in our Western culture that lure us away from faith in Christ. But He is sufficient for every need in every circumstance. Many people fall away from their faith because of the pressures involved in living life as a Stranger here.

If you are a person who has come to believe that Jesus is the sacrifice for your sin, have received His forgiveness and begun that new relationship, then the rest of this book is intended for you. The next two chapters deal with the heart of the personal conflict we engage in daily once we come to faith in Christ. It is a conflict every Christian experiences, whether you are new to faith in Christ, or have known Him for 50 years. The conflict is present every day. Understanding this conflict is critical to finding the answers to the questions in chapter one. Before we talk about the personal conflict, we will look at some general realities related to the conflict.

CHAPTER 7

The Underlying Conflict

⌘

"For we do not wrestle against flesh and blood, but against principalities, against powers, against the rulers of the darkness of this age, against spiritual hosts of wickedness in the heavenly places." (Ephesians 6:12)

As believers in Christ, we have God's Spirit within us. Our earthly nature continues to be utterly opposed to being influenced and moved toward living a life of God's righteousness. The result is a constant conflict between our new way of being and our old way of living. The new way is fueled by the Holy Spirit living within us. The old way is anchored in our physical being and empowered by the corruption of sin that is bound by our earthly existence. The old way is also encouraged and influenced by the principalities, powers of the spiritual world and world system and culture of the physical world around us.

As those who profess faith in Christ, we are daily faced with a conflict between two distinct and diverse ways of thinking and living. As Strangers in this world, the battle ground is our mind. The goal in the conflict is to influence our choices and the prize is our souls. The reborn spirit within us is in constant conflict with the sin nature bound in our physical bodies. This does not mean that our physical bodies are evil, as the Gnostics taught in the times of the Apostles and into the third century. It simply means that, until the third phase of our salvation occurs, we have a conflict going on inside of us between doing that which the Spirit within us is moving us to do and that which our bodies, which contain the corruption of sin, move us to do. It is the inherited desire to live apart from God, to be independent, that is at the root of our struggle to live a life that honors God as our Creator. Before we get into the inner war, we need to consider some broader aspects of the conflict.

Five spiritual realities lie behind the conflict in which we find ourselves. First, there is no negotiating with Satan. He is unrepentantly corrupt, and his influence is thoroughly corrupting. He is rotten to the core, the father of lies,[1] bent on stealing, killing and destroying[2] anything to do with Creator God and His relationship with His created beings. Satan is gleeful when he can make just one person deny God. He is ecstatic when he can nullify the testimony of even one believer. He drools with delight at the prospect of corrupting even one life, one soul. When he can deceive societies, or nations, he is at his highest state of euphoria. He thrives on division, hatred and the destruction of human life. There is nothing redeemable in him, nor in the hordes who follow him. They are destined for eternal damnation. To expect any sense of fair play or compassion from them is futile and foolish.

The second spiritual reality that lies behind this conflict for our souls is that Satan has already been defeated and judged.[3] Jesus made a public spectacle of the spiritual forces of this world after disarming them.[4] He completely conquered them. When Jesus died on the cross and rose from the dead, he won back the rights of the dominion that Adam and Eve forfeited through their disobedience. While we do not yet see the full effects of Jesus' victory in Creation, God will bring it about at the right time in human history.

The third spiritual reality behind this daily conflict is that the battlefield upon which this war is waged is within each individual human being. For those who have not yet come to faith in Christ, the challenge is about coming to a place of saving faith in Christ. For those who have made that decision to believe in Christ, the war is waged over how to live this life in obedience to God. Because the battle is an inner one, there is no neutral ground. We are either moving toward God, or away from Him. The choice is ours. This inner battle every believer faces is discussed in depth in chapter eight.

The fourth spiritual reality we must get a hold of is that God desires every human being to come into relationship with Himself. I have long believed that God is looking for an excuse to save, not a reason to condemn. The picture many people have of God waiting to zap them with a bolt of lightning is an effective lie of Satan. The Apostle John tells us that God is love.[5] God's love satisfied

God's justice and now, those who will choose to believe, will be rescued from eternal judgment. The justice of God, which demanded payment for humanity's sin, was satisfied by the death of Christ on the cross.[6] God is good and desires good for us, His creations.

The fifth spiritual reality is that God assures us we can find rest, even amid our struggles in this life. The writer of Hebrews wrote of a rest for the people of God.[7] This rest comes from faith in the Creator's promises and cessation of striving to earn relationship with God. Jesus said that, if we are burdened, we should take his work upon ourselves and He will give us rest.[8] Paul wrote that, even though he was in chains, the Gospel of Christ was unbounded and he had the strength to endure all things.[9] Paul endured many hardships for the Gospel, yet he lived in peace of spirit.

Though life can sometimes feel like a constant battle, we can find rest in Christ as we confront the works of darkness in our culture and resist our inner temptations and struggles while we work to fulfill God's purpose for our life. There is a way to live that allows us to have peace within ourselves through God's Spirit within us.

In one season of my life in the early 2000s, I was torn apart by my own failures, the unfounded accusations of several people in my life and the inability to bring legal resolution to a situation. I was angry, frustrated and scared for someone I could not help; someone for whom I had a duty to

90

protect and whom I loved deeply. As I expressed my anger at God and the situation, I heard only one thing in response. "I love you," was the message that came through to me clearly. It Was like God was wrapping His arms around me in my depressed, angry and helpless situation and assuring me He was in control. God did not reach into my situation and tell me what a loser I was, though that is what I felt. He reached into my life and told me how much He loved me. In that moment, my mind was confused, my emotions were raw. But, in my spirit, I sensed God's peace, acceptance and unconditional love. This did not happen just once, but numerous times over several months until the situation was resolved. It seemed like an eternity. But, in the end, God brought about a total victory and personal vindication. Such is the peace available to us through God's indwelling Spirit.

God desires that closeness for every one of you reading this. He also wants it with everyone you know. It has been my experience through many years of learning this Stranger's life that, while God is holy, He is also love. His love is not based on how we perform but is based on the acknowledgement that we will inevitably fail to perform. It is unconditional. It is also provisional in that He has provided the way to reestablish broken relationship with Himself – not just once, but as many times as we need it.

One way to understand the significance of the choice to follow Christ is to think in terms of stakeholders. A stakeholder is one who will either benefit or be negatively impacted, by any decision, endeavor, or activity. The idea is that there are individuals, or groups of individuals, in this war in which we find ourselves who will be impacted (in whatever way) by how we respond to the invitation to follow Christ. There are four stakeholders related to our individual decision to accept and follow Christ.

The first stakeholder is you and me. It is the individual who is making the choice to believe the historical evidence and testimony of believers who have gone before us. We will individually receive the Holy Spirit,[10] obtain acceptance in God's family,[11] and gain eternal life through our personal faith in Christ.[12] When a person makes the decision to trust in Christ, all the benefits we discussed in chapter six are theirs. As individual, unique creations, we have the most to gain by choosing faith in Christ and we have the most to lose by not choosing to place our faith in Christ.

The choice is clear: eternity with God or eternity apart from God. Eternity begins in this very moment. Before we made the decision to believe in Jesus and accept the forgiveness God offers us in Him, we were already living our eternity apart from God. When we were unbelievers, we may have seen God work in the lives of those around us, but we did not enjoy the intimate relationship with Him that we do now that we believe in Him. If we had stayed unbelievers, until this body of flesh dies, we would have continued to exist, but we would be apart from God for all eternity.[13]

In contrast, because we chose to believe in Jesus and receive the forgiveness God offers us in Christ, our eternity of living with God began in that moment. When this body of flesh dies, we will continue the eternal life we began in this life, but it will be without the corruption we experience in this earthly body. Rather than the unclear perception of God we often experience in this life, we will know Him then as we are now known by Him.[14] We will have a new, incorruptible body for all eternity.[15]

Clearly, the stakeholder with the most to gain or lose, is the individual human being. God desires a personal relationship with each one of His free will possessing creations.[16] That relationship starts here and now but continues for all eternity and only gets better when our time here is fulfilled.

The second stakeholder in this war is not one person, but a group of individuals. This group consists of all the people you and I have the potential to reach and impact during our lifetime. These people are in the various spheres of influence we belong to throughout our lives. There is the family sphere, work spheres and all the spheres of influence related to where we shop, work out, or attend church. Even one-time random encounters belong in this group of stakeholders. There are people in this life for whom you might be the only person they will listen to about Jesus. We are all unique and we each have our own way of communicating and connecting with others.

Many in this group of stakeholders may not even currently know they have a stake in our decision. It is often not clear for years. We have no idea who the people are that we will meet and potentially influence in our lifetime. We could meet someone for five minutes and say one thing that God uses to turn their thinking around and impact them for eternity. For others, we may know them for years and when we are gone, they might tell our family that we were instrumental in providing an example and testimony to them that changed their eternal destiny. We may never know we made that impact on them.

At my father's memorial service in 2006, there were several people who stood up and talked about how much Dad influenced their lives. I never knew Dad had that kind of impact on people. I doubt that he did either. He would have been humbled and honored to hear what many people said about him that day.

This second group of stakeholders is comprised of parents, children, cousins, aunts, uncles, grandparents, grandchildren, distant relatives, friends, the store clerk, coworkers, managers, people we attend church with, casual connections, business associates and more. Because this group includes all our spheres of influence throughout our lives, the list of potential members is almost limitless.

The result of our individual choices - both to believe in Christ for the forgiveness of our sins and our daily decisions to follow God impact the people of this stakeholder group to a degree that we cannot fully measure or predict. When we fail to follow God's plan for our own lives, people in this group could miss out on hearing our voice. I do not write to inspire guilt, so if you are feeling guilt as you read this, you should stop now and read Romans 8:1-2. We have all missed opportunities to be a positive influence in the lives of others. None of us can undo what we have done. Nor can we go back and do what we failed to do in the past. All we can do is accept God's clean slate for our life today and move forward with a renewed commitment to do better.

Conviction is drastically different from condemnation. The Holy Spirit's conviction is a loving revelation of wrongdoing and an invitation to repentance. When we respond to His conviction, the result is forgiveness and restoration of relationship. Condemnation is an often degrading, judgmental and fear inspiring statement or sensation that makes us feel like failures. Condemnation gives us the impression that, "God could never love one such as me." The Holy Spirit is always working for restoration of our lives and moving us toward relationship with our Creator; our loving, heavenly Father. The Holy Spirit never expresses contempt for us, but consistently communicates God's offer of forgiveness, unconditional love and call to righteousness.

Instead of inspiring condemnation for our failures, which we all have, this is written to draw our attention to the idea that we each have the power to influence the lives of others. How will you and I use that power? Will we use it to influence people to grow, seek God and become what God created them to be? Or, will we use our power of influence to lead people away from God, to wicked behavior and subsequent misery and judgment?

This second group of stakeholders whom each of us can influence toward God are waiting for us to live the life God has for us to live. How many of them will be in eternal relationship with God because of our obedience to Christ? No one knows. The only way to discover that is to live out the call and purpose our Creator designed each one of us to live. God created each one of us for something unique. It can only be fully discovered and have its greatest impact on others through our relationship with Christ.

The third stakeholder in the war for our souls is Satan and his kingdom of evil. Satan's stake in our lives is an extension of his rebellion against God. When he sought to displace God from his throne, Satan ended up cast out of God's presence. Satan's hatred of God and His created beings is almost beyond the capacity of human words explain; he is bent on the deception and destruction of all whom he can influence and, as a consequence, he is set apart for eternal damnation.[17] He lusts for human company in his eternal suffering.

Satan once enjoyed a position of prestige and honor in God's design, but his pride lifted him up in rebellion against God. God has judged him, cast him out of his position and now there is no space in his being for compassion, or mercy. Since we are created in God's image, Satan's goal is our allegiance to him. Personal allegiance to Satan was involved in one of the temptations of Christ.[18] If he cannot have our allegiance, he would see us destroyed. If he cannot destroy us, he would have us suffer. If he cannot cause us to suffer, he would work to render our influence ineffectual. If he cannot render our influence ineffectual, he would have us be confused and feeling inadequate. His victory comes when he can accomplish any one, or all, of those goals.

In 1977, Christian singer and song writer, Keith Green, released a song entitled, "No One Believes in Me Anymore."[19] The song was written from Satan's perspective and talked about how easy it is for him to operate when no one believes in him anymore. If people have the image of him as a little red being with horns and a pitchfork, he is happy. He has successfully marketed himself to our culture as a harmless superstition, or something that gives one chills at the movies. He does his best work when he is undetected.

The fourth stakeholder in the war for our souls is God himself. It was God's desire to have personal relationship with us that has made it possible for us to have relationship with Him in the first place. He is the initiator in the process. It cost Jesus everything to secure it for us. Consider for a moment what Jesus has done. He left heaven where He was revered by angels, in a relationship of perfect love and union with the Father and the Holy Spirit.[20] Paul wrote in Philippians 2:5-8 about the humility Christ took on during His life as a human male on Earth. Theologians tell us that Jesus gave up His divine prerogatives and lived his earthly life as one of us. Jesus' reliance upon God and His Spirit was complete and consistent as a human man. He lived as a man in submission to the Father through the power of the Spirit to show us the way to put God first in our lives.[21] In doing so, He became the unblemished Lamb of God – the Passover Lamb – who paid for the sins of the whole world. In Jesus' hours on the cross, His Father turned His back on Him[22] and poured out the wrath and judgment for our sins upon Him.[23]

God – Father, Son and Holy Spirit – were willing to endure this sacrifice because of the great love our Creator has for each one of us. It is His desire that all of us come to know the truth and are saved from an eternity outside of relationship with God.

God has shown His heart for His people throughout the whole Bible. Reading through the Old Testament, we read repeatedly that God desires His people to repent from their sins and turn to Him. He wants to be our God and for us to be His people.[24] God is a Being who enjoys relationship. There is perfect unity in the Godhead (Father, Son and Holy Spirit) and He desires intimate relationship with each one of the free will human beings He created.[25]

God desires a people who come to Him of their own free will.[26] Since the beginning, He has sought out human beings that will enter relationship with him. He involves himself with those who move toward Him.[27] His motivation is a completely unselfish love for each individual. God's love has the best interests of the loved one at heart.

We tend to look at our relationship with God only in the context of this life. We frequently fail to realize that God is working in us with an eternal purpose, not just a purpose for this life. Ultimately, God will have us enjoy relationship with Him forever. Our physical life is precious to Him. So are the timing and circumstances of our passing from this hindered relationship with Him into our unfettered relationship with Him.[28]

In this life, what is best for us from an eternal perspective is not what we think is best from our temporal perspective. Satan frequently uses the distortion of what is best for us to bring doubt and distrust of our Savior to our hearts. Remaining grounded in the love of Christ is critical as we engage in the war raging around us.

With these principles and understanding of the stakeholders involved, we can look at how this age-old conflict works out in our daily life as a Stranger. It is safe to say that it is a spiritual hand-to-hand combat.

CHAPTER 8
This, Is War

CR

*"I do not understand what I do. For
what I want to do I do not do, but
what I hate I do. So, I find this law at
work: Although I want to do good,
evil is right there with me. For in my
inner being I delight in God's law; but
I see another law at work in me,
waging war against the law of my mind
and making me a prisoner of the law
of sin at work within me." (Romans
7:15, 21-23)*

Paul wrote to the Romans about the struggle he faced in his life serving Christ. Every person dedicated to growing in a relationship with Christ will face similar struggles. It is the battle over which path we will follow, what impulses we will allow to shape and move our lives. Paul's use of the term "waging war" in the passage above is intended to illustrate the nature of the conflict we embrace daily. War in first century Rome was a personal, often brutal business. Most combat was face-to-face in a kill or be killed confrontation.

The conflict in which we find ourselves immersed involves interactions. As we discussed in chapter two, we were created with a body and a spirit so that we can interact with the physical and spiritual worlds around us. There are also interactions going on within ourselves. These

101

internal interactions involve our soul, spirit and body.

In chapter two, we looked at this diagram that illustrated how human beings are put together with spirit in the center, body as an outer circle and soul as a circle in between. While this diagram is an excellent illustration of the makeup of humans, there is another diagram that better illustrates the conflict in which we are engaged. In the first diagram, spirit is shown at the center of our being because it is from the depths of our being that we know God. It is also from the depths of our being that the fruit of God's work in us springs forth.

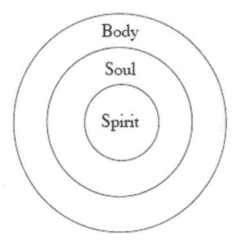

This new illustration shows the connections between ourselves and the worlds in which we live. Soul is at the center of this diagram because soul is at the center of the war we are fighting. It is our will that both the spiritual and physical worlds are working to influence. Soul holds the responsibility for everything in our lives, because it is in our souls that we choose our actions and our words.

We are made alive in our inner being through the indwelling Holy Spirit. We can only know God, who is Spirit, through our human spirit because the things of God are "spiritually discerned".[1] God's influence in our lives is spiritual and comes to us through our spirit. Though He also influences us through other human beings and His Word, His direct communication to us is predominantly through our spirit within. Of course, there are always exceptions, such as when God spoke to Balaam through a donkey[2] or to Moses out of a burning bush.[3]

Our spirit never sleeps and can receive from God even when we are not aware of what is happening. Our spirit can be strengthened, even when the mind is not involved; reading God's word, worshipping the Lord, biblical mediation and prayer, all fuel our spirit.

While conscious, we constantly receive input from the physical world around us. The input from the physical world all comes to us through our physical body. Our five senses perceive inputs from culture, peer pressure, media, social norms and the cravings of our own bodies. These are all influences we constantly process and use to make our decisions. Every input from the physical environment passes through the brain and is available to the soul and spirit for evaluation and internal influence.

This diagram also shows the influence of Satan as coming from the Earthly realm and directed at our soul. While Satan is a spiritual being, he has been cast down to the Earth. Unlike our Creator, Satan is not capable of being present everywhere. His realm is of the Earthly region. For the believer in Christ, Satan cannot possess, that is live inside the individual. He can only attempt to oppress the believer, bring confusion to our minds and work in the world through circumstances and individuals around us. He will try to bring pressure and seeks to influence us, but he is limited to doing those things from outside our being. He cannot control the believer in Jesus as he can a person who does not have God's Holy Spirit living in them.

God created us with the ability to reason. We are constantly processing information and reasoning out how we will respond to the information we are receiving. Impulses from our body, our emotions and memories, as well as physical sensations and spiritual perceptions from the world around us are continuously monitored and processed as to subject and priority. While much of this sorting and categorizing is subconscious, we make many conscious choices every day.

A third diagram illustrates how everything is focused on the soul and more precisely on the will. Everything we say and do is the result of a choice. Every impulse, every impression, every bit of sensing pass through the body or spirit and gets processed in the soul. The will is involved in everything going on inside of us except for those processes that are involuntary, such as maintaining a heartbeat, or a reflex action. Even so, by force of will we are able to temporarily stop some vital processes, such as breathing so we do not drown when we are under water.

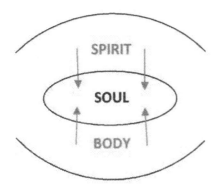

Our bodies constantly seek satisfaction. Our bodies are not rational at all. They seek only to have their needs met. Hunger, thirst, the need for comfort of temperature, sexual desire, the desire for pleasing sounds and scents; these impulses are constantly being sent to the brain where they move through the decision-making process.

Something as simple as an itch on our ankle goes through this process. The soul picks up the signal from the brain that there is an itch on the ankle. In most cases, the will allows the body to respond and scratch the itch as a reflex action. But there are times the will overrules the urge of the body. For instance, special forces soldiers in a critical situation may choose to not scratch the itch over concern that their movement could give away their position to an enemy. The will frequently overrules the signal from the body in matters of survival, good taste, or for moral reasons. Through our will, we have the power to control every part of our being.

In Psalm 103:1, David exhorted his soul to praise the Lord. From his will, he commanded his soul and all that is within himself to offer praise (a spiritual activity) to the Lord. In Psalm 63:4, David says, "Thus I will bless You while I live; I will lift up my hands in Your name." David exercised his will to give his body direction on how to praise the Lord. David's praise, a spiritual action, was initiated when David exercised his will over his body, his spirit and his soul.

Inputs from the spiritual world become known by our souls through our spirits. Spiritual awareness is something that can be developed but is much less natural for us because our natural inclination is toward the dominant presence of the physical world around us. While the spiritual world is just as real, we are not normally trained to perceive it. Things we term as a sixth sense or following our "gut" are perceptions of our spirits. Before we come to Christ, these spiritual capacities are not functioning under the guidance of the Holy Spirit. If they are functioning at all, they are distorted and self-oriented. Once we come to faith in Christ, these spiritual capacities can be put to work by the Holy Spirit for the purposes for which God originally intended.

In Acts 8:9-25, we are introduced to a man named Simon. Simon lived in Samaria, the region north of Jerusalem. He was a sorcerer who had a large following among the people living in Samaria. Simon demonstrated great power among the people of his region by performing signs and wonders. His reputation was well known by all the people. Because of his power, people from all over the region listened to him and saw him as one whose wisdom was to be heeded. He was revered by the people and likely profited from his perceived spiritual abilities.[4]

Philip was one of seven men chosen as deacons of the Jerusalem church in Acts 6:5. When he went through Samaria preaching the Gospel of the Kingdom and the good news of Jesus, not only did many of the people in Samaria believe the message, but Simon also came to faith in Christ.[5] When the apostles in Jerusalem heard the news of Philip's success, they sent Peter and John to Samaria to help him. Upon arriving, they prayed for the new believers and the Holy Spirit was given to them.[6]

Simon, seeing the way the power of the Apostles was displayed and that the Holy Spirit came upon people when the Apostles prayed, offered to give Peter and John money if he could have this same power.[7] Peter's response was something I'm sure Simon did not expect. He told Simon that his heart was not right with God because he thought the gift of God could be purchased with money.[8]

Six things stand out to me in this episode in the life of the early church. First, Simon was a spiritually connected person before he came to Christ; he was a sorcerer. The Greek word in Acts 8:9 means "wise man" and was used of the wise men who came with gifts at Jesus' birth. The meaning can also include calling on spirits, incantations, performing magic and witchcraft. The text says that the people of Samaria heeded Simon and said that he was, "the great power of God".[9] There was something happening with Simon more than wisdom. He apparently displayed something beyond the physical realm that caused people to say he had the power of God. Simon's spiritual connection promoted his stature and personal profit in the physical world. His spiritual gifts were self-serving.

The second thing we see in this text is that, whatever Simon demonstrated, it was nothing compared to the power displayed when Philip came to preach or when the Apostles prayed for people to receive the gift of the Holy Spirit. People were freed from spiritual bondage and healed of physical ailments.[10] The change was so dramatic that joy filled the city,[11] which is often the case when bondage is broken. Simon's self-serving prowess in the region was displaced by the power of God working through the disciples.

The third thing to notice is that, even though the people came to faith in Christ and many were healed and delivered from the bondage of evil spirits, there was still something missing in their lives that God wanted them to have. The Apostles came and prayed so that the people who previously believed were filled with the Holy Spirit. There was an additional dimension of God's gifting from the Holy Spirit that simply believing the message did not provide.

The fourth thing we notice is that, while Simon also believed Philip's message, he was still caught up in his previous mindset. When Simon saw Peter and John lay hands on people and saw that they were filled with the Holy Spirit, he desired that same power. Though Simon had come to believe in Christ, he had not yet made the transition from his previous way of thinking to that of self-denial and following the Spirit. When Phillip and the Apostles showed up, the real power of God came with them. Simon wanted this power too so he would not lose the prestige and income he had established. It takes time to develop a Christ-centered mind set and the road there is often bumpy.

The fifth thing to notice in this scene is that there was something beyond the physical going on between Peter and Simon. Simon was operating on a material, financial level. Peter looked beyond the material into the spiritual realm and called Simon out on the condition of his heart. The ability Peter had to look at the heart of the issue was not from his own ability. It was the gift of the Holy Spirit. The Spirit worked through Peter to illuminate the condition of Simon's heart.

The sixth and final thing to notice is that Simon started out as a pagan, self-serving, self-promoting man who did what he did for personal gain and prestige. Through events in the physical world, a display of God's power and his own internal conviction, Simon became a man who respected God's power and wanted to do the right thing. Acts 8:24 says that when Peter scolded Simon for his attitude, Simon asked Peter to pray for him that none of these things would come upon him. To me, his reaction to Peter indicates that Simon was now open to correction and instruction.

All of us are broken and come to Christ broken. The egg of our make-up is cracked; our yoke and white are scrambled. We are not all broken to the same degree, but we are all broken. Like the rest of our being, our spirits are flawed because of the power of sin in all of humanity. We are separated from God, but through the work of His Spirit, Jesus reaches into our world to take us from where we are and moves us into a relationship with our Creator. When God's Spirit comes to live inside us at the point of salvation, we are reborn spiritually and He begins to restore an awareness we can either facilitate, neglect, or suppress. It is the Holy Spirit who empowers our spiritual perceptions and sharpens our spiritual skills through the gifts He gives to us. Effectively living the Stranger's life requires us to make choices and take action that foster our spiritual growth, but it is the Holy Spirit who brings results.

Satan is happy when we are unaware of our spiritual nature so we do not seek our Creator or grow in our relationship with God. Satan wins when he keeps us ignorant, distracted, or unmotivated to pursue the relationship with our Creator that Jesus purchased for us. Therefore, he works to deceive and confuse our reasoning and coerce our will so that we will choose to not follow God. In doing so, his goal is to pressure us, or seduce us, to live contrary to God's purpose for our lives.

Satan also works to diminish our sense of value and the value of human life in general. He tries to make us feel undeserving of God's grace and favor. But it is not at all about deserving God's favor. It is about recognizing that God's favor is given based on faith in Jesus. We will never deserve God's love, but we can receive God's forgiveness and live in His love through faith.

God also wants to influence our will. But where Satan attempts to deceive and coerce us, God uses love, truth and reason to persuade us. Satan attempts to manipulate our choices through any means available to him. He would overpower our free will if he could. God will never violate our free will but will convict us with truth in love to influence us to make right choices. God will never impose His will on us but will show us the consequences of our wrong choices, while allowing us to decide for ourselves.

112

Our internal interactions are the means through which our will is influenced. One powerful internal interaction is habit. Habits are behaviors, or ways of thinking, that are nearly automatic. Habit can be a powerful force for good or bad. Just as smoking, or overeating are bad habits, regularly brushing our teeth and getting enough exercise are good habits. Breaking ingrained habits or creating new habits can take time. God will give us grace to work through the process of building good habits to replace bad habits. If we are to break habits, become more like Jesus in our daily life and make a difference in the world around us, it will be because we made a choice to change and to allow the Holy Spirit to do His work in us and through us. It will require some willful effort on our part to be successful.

Our choices are not only influenced by the Holy Spirit within us, but by the world around us. Culture, friends, family, social norms, legal systems, work environment, media, social connections and more, all provide input to our souls to filter and consider at an almost constant rate. Even our own emotions add a dimension of influence to our choices. How many times have you heard we should not make an emotional decision? All of these influences either support a faith in Christ and living a life that reflects His life in us, or they influence us to lose faith and become indifferent, or even hostile, to the new way of life to which our Creator calls us. Many influences are subtle and go nearly unnoticed if we do not pay attention.

Think of a familiar room in your life. Perhaps it is your bedroom, or kitchen, or office. Do you have that pictured in your mind? Suppose I wanted to change the color of the room without you noticing. If I came in and changed the color while you were gone, you would most likely notice the change when you came back. Depending on the difference in color, it might take you a few seconds to a matter of minutes to notice the difference, but you would likely notice the change quickly.

Now, suppose I am not in a hurry, but I am committed to accomplishing my goal. I could come in and slowly change the color, maybe even use an atomizer to ever so slowly change the color. It might take me months, or even years, but I don't care. I simply want to change the color without you noticing. In time, I would succeed. You would likely not consciously notice, though you may sense something different. It is likely that one day you would realize the change and wonder how that happened. If I don't care how long it takes me, I could likely change the color of the room without you noticing.

The same thing can happen in our spiritual lives. Slowly, often insidiously, the influences of a godless culture work on our lives through media, social norms, peer pressure, disappointments, frustrated expectations, long lasting trials, extended illnesses and other life events can erode our faith in God and our commitment to living in Christ. Satan's most effective work is done in the dark. It is accomplished outside our conscious recognition.

Satan effectively works through the culture around us, especially when the culture is not generally accepting of faith in Christ. In twenty-first century, Western culture, media plays a large role in influencing our public discourse and acceptable practices. Celebrity worship, the unbridled quest for riches, the desire for ease in life, constant comparisons between the haves and have not's all work to bring discontent and cause us to question God's promises to us in Christ. This is the subtlety of Satan. He tries to work in ways that people won't even notice that he is the one behind it.

We do not need to live in constant fear of being influenced or having the color of our room changed without us noticing. But we do need to be on guard for those things that negatively impact our living a life in relationship with God. It is always better to be proactive and let the Holy Spirit guide us than to be paranoid and fearful. By that, I mean that there are things we can do to maintain a vital relationship with God. In John 15:4, Jesus said to, "Abide in Me." We will look at some things we can do to abide in Christ in chapter ten.

Every impulse, every input, everything we see, hear, touch and smell is processed in our minds and souls. Throughout history, Christians

115

have leaned toward walling themselves off from society so that they could be holy before God. But what did Jesus do? He sat down with sinners, some of the worst of society. From a position of security in God, He gave them forgiveness, healing and life. That is what we are called to do as well. Jesus showed us the way. It is something that is beyond human effort, but it is not beyond us if we are filled with God's Spirit, living in obedience to His call and following His guidance.

Paul put it this way in Galatians 5:16-18, "Walk in the Spirit and you shall not fulfill the lust of the flesh. For the flesh lusts against the Spirit and the Spirit against the flesh; and these are contrary to one another, so that you do not do the things that you wish. But if you are led by the Spirit, you are not under the law." Paul goes on to list what living according to the corruption of the sin nature looks like. Before we came to Christ, we unconsciously followed the desires of our sin nature. It was all we knew. Now that we have God's Spirit within us, if we see things like adultery, fornication, uncleanness, lewdness, idolatry, sorcery, hatred, contentions, jealousies, outbursts of wrath, selfish ambitions, dissensions, heresies, envy, murders, drunkenness, revelries and the like,[12] we need to recognize they come from the corrupt nature within us and seek God's help in changing.

As Christians, we have the power to confront these ways of thinking and living, but it involves our choices, our free will. It involves developing new habits that result in getting to know God on a personal level. God will help us, but we must want His help. He knows our hearts and if we are simply putting up a front on Sunday morning, but not genuinely seeking God, He knows it and we will likely continue to be frustrated in our growth. We cannot successfully put a mask on for God because He looks at the heart, not the exterior.

When we come to Christ, we have been trained by the ways of the world around us. Like Simon earlier in this chapter, we all have ways of thinking and living that need to change. Most of these ways of thinking will not change overnight, but as we grow in our knowledge of God, how He works and as we allow the Holy Spirit to do His work within us, we will see changes in our lives. God calls us to a process that will continue until we cast aside this body of flesh and receive our incorruptible body.

As we grow in our relationship with God, we will see the results of His Spirit's working in us more evident in our daily lives. The results will show up as, "love, joy, peace, longsuffering [patience], kindness, goodness, faithfulness, gentleness, [and] self-control."[13] The Holy Spirit will always move us toward Christ. When we put God and the pursuit of His right living as the priority in our lives, God steps in and gives us everything we need.[14] We will most likely not have everything we want, either materially, or emotionally, but we will have everything we need if we persist and do not give up. We may not see things happen on our timetable, but God will always move in our lives to fulfill the purposes for which He saves us. Always!

There are many encouragements in the Bible about perseverance. Realistically, it takes a lot of courage and fortitude to live God's way as a Stranger in this world. God never promised it would be easy. In fact, he said we would need to pick up our cross and follow Him.[15] A cross is not a place of comfort, but of surrender. While we may look at the cross and see the place where the penalty for our sins was paid, for Jesus it was a place of suffering. For us, the cross can be a symbol of forgiveness and restoration. For Christ, it was the place of complete surrender and sacrifice. Jesus' call to take up our cross is a call to sacrificial living, but it is not a heavy burden, for the One who carried His cross will empower us to carry ours.[16] Not everyone is willing to heed His call, but we all have the opportunity and the capacity to follow Him. Thankfully, God has made allowance for even those who sin after coming to faith in Christ to find restoration to relationship with God.

None of us are without sin. Setting ourselves up as more righteous in our own right as someone else is a deception. If any of us think we can stand before God in our own righteousness, we are deceived.[17] We all need God's grace and mercy daily. It takes humility to seek God and His kingdom first. Pride and self-absorption are the deadliest attitudes.

While there is a healthy pride that contributes to a proper view of who we are and what we have accomplished, the type of pride that is destructive is the pride that puts "me, myself and I" first. This type of pride looks down on others who are perceived to be in a lower station in life, or who commit certain sins. This type of pride is the antithesis of loving our neighbor as ourselves. Pride is the attitude that caused Lucifer to fall from heaven. It can cause our fall as well. No wonder scripture tells us to guard our hearts[18] and to watch our life and doctrine closely.[19] If we are not vigilant, we can easily be drawn away from God's intended life of grace.

However we choose to live our lives, it is the result of our choices. If we produce a life of fleshly pursuits, it is our choice. If our life is filled with the fruit of a life lived following the Spirit of God, it too is the result of our choices. Either we will allow God to work in our lives, or the corruption of sin will be the predominant force working in our lives.

None of us are immune to sin's corruption. Not you, not me, not our pastor, not our priest, not our rabbi, not the Pope, not our boss, not our spouse, not our kids, not our neighbor. None of us can deal with the power and consequence of sin on our own. If we are to live a life that pleases God, we will accept His free offer of forgiveness and make choices every day that allow Him to shape us into the person He designed us to be. When we fall short — and we will fall short of God's ideal — we have the power to turn around, seek His grace and forgiveness and move forward.

It is time now to look at the deeper answers to the questions in chapter one.

CHAPTER 9

Answers

✂

"There is a way that seems right to a man,

But its end is the way of death."
Proverbs 14:12

"If any of you lacks wisdom, you should ask God, who gives generously to all without finding fault and it will be given to you." James 1:5

In chapter one, we looked at a series of questions from three events in the life of Jesus. You may have come up with questions of your own as you read through these events. In chapters two through eight, I shared some of my thought process as I attempted to satisfy my own question of how we crucify the deeds of the sin nature. Remarkably, every one of these questions boils down to one, core answer and gets to the very heart of why Jesus came to Earth, lived a sinless life, died a horrific death and rose from the dead victorious over all that plagues humanity.

The first event we looked at in chapter one was from John chapters 7 - 8. In this section, Jesus had several confrontations with the Jewish, religious leaders in Jerusalem during the Feast of

Tabernacles. The questions we asked regarding these confrontations were: How could those who were supposed to be the educated guides and leaders of Israel – those who had knowledge of the scriptures and supposedly the relationship with God – how could they not see the truth in what Jesus was saying? What made these teachers of the Law so closed to the possibility of Jesus being the Messiah?

At Jesus' so-called trial, scripture says that even Pilot saw that the leaders were jealous of Jesus,[1] but he was compelled by his priorities as Roman governor and by the Jews to release Barabbas and condemn Jesus.[2] The Jewish leaders saw masses of people following Jesus.[3] Jesus' appeal among the people was that he was genuine, not condescending. He had authority and did not speak like the teachers of the Law.[4] His mission was to set people free, not to keep them in bondage to gratify his own ego.[5] He upset the power base the leaders had built up for themselves and even inherited by their position in society. Their position and authority thrived on oppressing people through a rigid system of religious rules.

So, in response to our questions, jealousy, closed mindedness and feeling threatened, all contributed to the decision to reject Jesus and have him killed. But there was something deeper going on. These issues were the symptoms of the root issue happening in the lives of the Jewish leaders. The root issue was that their priority in life was themselves, not a personal relationship with their

Creator. Jesus said that, if God was their Father, they would love him.[6] It comes down to the age-old issue we saw in the Garden with Adam and Eve. We saw the same human shortcoming all through the history of Israel as recorded in the Bible. It is our natural tendency as human beings to put a relationship with God dead last in our priorities. Power, prestige, comfort, satisfaction and human companionship all vie for our focus and work to push out a focus on our Creator and doing what pleases Him. We avoid humility and fail to acknowledge God for who He is.

Religion is not relationship. Religion is a manmade structure that all too often puts the focus on a list of dos and don'ts and on actions as humans. Religion is frequently used as a way for us to show God how good we are. It all too often clouds our view of God and blinds us to what God's purpose is for our lives. Religion focuses on the externals, but God wants our hearts devoted to Him.[7] The religious leaders of Jesus' time were more focused on their standing with the people and Rome, than they were concerned about their standing with God. Most of them failed to recognize God, even when He was standing right in front of them. At the root of the choices the Jewish leaders made and of their jealousy, was this propensity of human beings to focus on everything but God.

The leaders themselves were trapped in a religious system that fed their egos and gave them prestige. The adage that power corrupts is true. The leaders of Jesus' day were drunk with the results of the religious control they exercised over the people. The system filled their lives with material provision as well as prestige and influence over masses of people. In the end, when Messiah confronted them, it was easier to make every effort to hold on to what they had in the physical world, than to be challenged to open their eyes to what was happening in the spiritual realm. Though some leaders, such as Nicodemus, appear to have believed in Jesus as Messiah,[8] most remained trapped in a dead religious system. Ever since that one, poor choice of Adam and Eve, human beings have been desperately broken. Regrettably, most choose to dismiss the only cure God has provided to regenerate what He originally intended for His human creations.

The second event in the life of Jesus from chapter one was from John, chapter 6. Jesus talked about being the Manna from Heaven and that his followers had to eat his flesh and drink his blood. The questions we asked at the end of this section were: What was it that caused so many of Jesus' disciples to leave him? Why could they not grasp what he was trying to say? Was there a connection between Jesus' observation that the crowds were following him just because he fed them and their willingness to leave him so quickly?

Early on in this encounter with the crowds, in John 6:26, Jesus said to the people who followed him from across the lake, "Most assuredly, I say to you, you seek Me, not because you saw the signs, but because you ate of the loaves and were filled" (John 6:26). The crowd was focused on their physical needs. This is key for this passage because, when Jesus started talking about eating his flesh and drinking his blood, he was not advocating cannibalism.[9] Rather, He was referring to something Jewish people were very familiar with in their culture and practice.

When Jesus ate the Passover with his disciples the night before he was crucified, he said that the bread was his body and the wine was his blood.[10] Per the rules of the Passover, this cup was the third cup of the meal and was taken after supper. The third cup is the cup of redemption. It was the cup Jesus referred to as, "This cup is the new covenant in My blood, which is shed for you".[11] Jesus took a long standing, Jewish Passover tradition and assigned a new covenant significance to it. So, when Jesus told the people who were following him in John 6 that they should eat his flesh and drink his blood, he was referring to a spiritual truth that would be instituted as part of the new covenant God was making with his people. In truth, the Passover celebration had been looking forward to the sacrifice of Jesus for more than 1,400 years to a covenant that would remove the sin of the people once and for all time.[12]

Another thing that preconditioned many people in the crowd to not understand what Jesus was saying is that there was a rigorous opposition to Roman rule in Israel in Jesus' time. People were looking for a political and military deliverer, not a suffering Messiah that would deliver them from their spiritual bondage. It would only be about 35 to 40 years from this time that Rome would demolish Jerusalem and crush the Jewish rebellion in the region. The seeds of that rebellion were sprouting during the lifetime of Jesus. This very crowd was ready to make him king by force to push the Jewish nationalistic agenda forward.[13] Their focus was on human agendas, not God's agenda.

The focus of the individuals in this crowd were on their physical needs and on a physical solution to Roman oppression. The last thing they were thinking of is a spiritual message in what Jesus was saying to them. Remember, the things of God are spiritually discerned.[14] Jesus stated that His words were spirit and life.[15] The people in this crowd heard things from Jesus they could not process within the framework of their religious and political realities. The things Jesus was teaching simply did not compute. Rather than do the work to question and search for truth and understanding, they walked away.

Facing the truth about ourselves is challenging. It is especially challenging when we are required to admit we are in the wrong. Humility does not come easily to us. Acknowledging God for who He is, looking past all the supposed good arguments against Him and following the spiritual impulse that testifies to our souls of the truth is not something every human being can do. But if we desire to be in relationship with our Creator, searching for answers to the hard questions is something we must do.

When we get to a point in our search for God that the answers to our questions are not easy to understand, the typical response is to go back to what we understand best. What we know best is not the spiritual response, but the response based on the physical world around us. Growing in our spiritual lives is challenging work. Not everyone is willing to put forth the effort to grow in their spiritual understanding. It takes discipline to focus our soul on the spiritual solution. Much of the crowd from this event were not the type of people to pursue spiritual truth. They were looking for a physical solution to a problem that was rooted in the spiritual realm. That is, their problem was the lack of relationship with their Creator, but they were so focused on the material provision, they could not see the spiritual provision available to them to meet their unperceived spiritual needs.

There were some who stuck around and sought the truth. Look at the response of Peter to Jesus' question to the twelve disciples about whether they too would leave him. John 6:68 says, "But Simon Peter answered Him, 'Lord, to whom shall we go? You have the words of eternal life.'" The Twelve may not have gotten everything Jesus taught, but they did get that they needed to hang around until they understood. They recognized that Jesus is Messiah and that there would be things they did not understand. They hung around until they got it and did not let their ignorance, prejudices, or lack of understanding get in the way of getting to know Jesus. Hanging around is critical to abiding in Christ. Sometimes, it is the best we can do.

The third event in the life of Jesus we looked at in chapter one was from Mark chapter 9. The same event is also recorded in Luke 9:28-43 and Matthew 16:28 - 17:21. The questions we asked at the end of that section were: What about this situation was different that the disciples could not cast out the demon? What about prayer and fasting facilitates casting out demons? What qualities were missing from the disciples' lives that prayer and fasting would strengthen? Are there some victories in the spirit that require the application of spiritual disciplines to become real in our lives? What about prayer in Jesus' life made it possible for him to cast out this demon, while the disciples could not?

As you may recall from our earlier discussion, the disciples were sent out to cast out demons, heal the sick and preach the Kingdom prior to this encounter.[16] Yet, in this situation, they could not cast it out. Jesus seemed irritated at their lack of faith.[17]   While there are many instances in the New Testament we see Jesus say something like, "Your faith has made you well," in this passage, Jesus looked at those who failed to cast out the spirit and heal the boy and rebuked them for their lack of faith. This lack of faith on the part of the disciples is the crucial component. Jesus said in Mark 9:29, "This kind can come out by nothing but prayer and fasting." Jesus points to two key disciplines of the Christian life that spiritually mature people have pointed to through the ages as being keys to seeing the power of God's Kingdom working in and through them. Those keys are prayer and fasting.

The answer to the first question about what was different in this situation is two-fold. The first part of the answer is that the demon was different. In Ephesians 6:12, Paul writes that we do not wrestle against flesh and blood, but against principalities, against powers, against the rulers of the darkness of this age, against spiritual hosts of wickedness in the heavenly places." As in any organization there is a hierarchy in the realm of Satan. When Jesus said, "This kind," he was making a distinction from other kinds of demons.

The second part of the answer that made this instance different is this is the first time we see the disciples confronted by Jewish leaders. The scribes were arguing with the disciples. The fact that there was a staunch resistance in the physical realm likely caused the disciples to lose focus. They had not yet developed the spiritual discipline to remain focused on the provision of the Spirit in the face of such opposition. They lacked the spiritual maturity they would later develop as we see in the Book of Acts when at least Peter and John stood up to the opposition of the Jewish leaders.[18]

Looking at the life of Jesus, there are many times in the Gospels where He left the crowds and prayed alone. Luke 5:15-16 says, "...and great multitudes came together to hear and to healed by Him of their infirmities. So, He Himself often withdrew into the wilderness and prayed." There is a strong connection between the fact that Jesus frequently went away to pray and commune with His Father and Jesus' massively successful healing and deliverance ministry.

Prayer is a powerful tool to increase our spiritual awareness and aptitudes. If prayer was something Jesus did regularly and he coupled prayer with casting out this demon, it makes sense that there is something to be gained in prayer that allows us to more completely fulfill our mission in Christ. Prayer with fasting is a way for us to focus on humbling ourselves before God and breaking down the work of the corruption of sin on our being. Fasting tells the physical being, it is not in control.

In His earthly life, Jesus made a practice of communion with His Father through the indwelling Holy Spirit. Because of this, He could cast out this demon and many others. While the disciples had not yet been able to do so at the time of this event, we read throughout the book of Acts that they reached the point in their lives where they did exercise authority over demons. Communion with God through prayer also helps the Stranger to stay focused on the Spirit and not be distracted by human or intellectual arguments. Regular prayer from a sincere and submitted heart, coupled with fasting, is an effective way to build spiritual strength and awareness.

Here, Jesus intimates that prayer and fasting are required for certain acts of service and ministry. The disciples had not yet developed their spiritual lives to the point they could handle this situation. To their credit, they asked Jesus for clarification and guidance.

The bottom line in all three of these situations is that human beings inherit a natural inclination to reject the spiritual aspect of life as it relates to having a personal relationship with our Creator. This is due primarily to two things. The fact that the physical realm dominates our awareness is the first reason. The second reason is that, due to sin's corruption, we are naturally self-focused and prideful. It is hard to humble ourselves and acknowledge our Creator as our Lord. God has initiated contact with humanity through creation, natural law and the life and work of Jesus Christ. We can either respond with acceptance and a sincere desire to know Him, or we can follow the natural inclination of our sin nature and reject Him. Our responses are too often distorted, such as in the three events we have looked at here. We can embrace religion, prestige and influence as the Jewish leaders did. Or, as the crowd did in the second event, we can focus on having our physical needs met. Or, we can fail to be disciplined in our spiritual lives and live in a way that we are limited in our ability to conquer our enemy and live victoriously. As we saw previously, Satan and his hordes are hard at work providing all kinds of distractions and deceptions in life. However many impulses we have working against us, we always have the choice of how we will respond and how we will live.

It comes down to giving the spiritual aspect of life its due attention and making it the priority it needs to be. The influence of the physical world around us can be overpowering. There is much we must set aside from the physical world if we are to be people who open ourselves up to the life changing work of the Holy Spirit. The Stranger's life is truly a life of discipline and choosing a different set of priorities.

We can attempt to push God aside and avoid relationship with Him as Israel did when they asked for a king, or we try to set ourselves up as God over our own lives, denying our need for a Savior and for our Creator, we can even over-focus on the physical world around us and get caught up in the material world. The bottom line is that, as human beings, we naturally tend to move away from a spiritual connection with our Creator. It is the corrupt nature within us that moves us in this direction. But God calls us. He woos us. He desires relationship with us. He holds out the offer of relationship, but only on His terms. How often we turn our backs to Him and go our own way. Truly, it is by His grace that we turn to Him and are saved. God is calling each one of us. Are you listening? Am I listening? Or, are we closing the door in His face?

Let us be men and women who allow the Holy Spirit to do His work in us, so that He can work through us. In the next chapter, we explore some things we can do proactively to allow God to shape our lives.

CHAPTER 10

On Moving Forward

ଔ

*"Therefore, we also, since we are
surrounded by so great a cloud of
witnesses, let us lay aside every weight
and the sin which so easily ensnares
us and let us run with endurance the
race that is set before us, ² looking
unto Jesus, the author and finisher of
our faith, who for the joy that was set
before Him endured the cross,
despising the shame and has sat down
at the right hand of the throne of
God." Hebrews 12:1-2*

*"I have fought the good fight, I have
finished the race, I have kept the
faith." 2 Timothy 4:7*

In the final analysis, we will overcome the
impulses of our sin nature by focusing upon and
learning to live in relationship with the Spirit of our
Creator. I am confident none of us will ever be
perfect at it this side of heaven. Every saint in the
Bible had their flaws. We should expect no less. But
we do not engage in this conflict alone. God has
given us His Word, His Spirit and each other. To
love one another means to build each other up – to
help each other navigate this life as a Stranger. One
interesting thing is that the more we help others
overcome, the more we help ourselves.

Living the Stranger's life in some ways is like gardening. If we ignore our garden, weeds will grow and use up the nutrition in the soil making it impossible to grow a good crop. On the other hand, if we take care of the garden by tilling the soil, using adequate fertilizer, watering regularly and pulling the weeds as they develop, we will reap a bountiful harvest with enough to share with our family, friends and neighbors. We plant the seed, take care of the environment for the seed and the process of life our Creator put into place makes the seed grow and produce a harvest. God causes the increase, but we too have a vital role to play in the process.

The corruption of our human nature is like weeds in the garden of our soul. We don't need to do a thing to get the sin nature to produce weeds in our lives. In contrast, Galatians 5:22 lists the fruit of the Spirit as, " love, joy, peace, longsuffering [patience], kindness, goodness, faithfulness, gentleness, self-control [self-discipline]." The fruit of the Spirit is not something we control, but it is something we can help to grow in our lives. We can also prevent it from being produced in our lives. Like a good harvest in our garden, the fruit of the Spirit growing in our lives is the result of specific choices and effort on our part. God has put a process in place spiritually, just as he has with physical seeds, to cause the fruit of the Spirit to develop in the lives of those who seek Him and who cultivate an environment where the Spirit can work within us.

We saw in chapter seven that we need to be on our guard to protect our souls from those influences that work to move our choices away from a relationship with God. In this chapter, we will look at some things we can do proactively to keep the garden of our lives prepared to produce a good harvest for the Lord. If we want a harvest of good results, we must be intentional about spiritual disciplines in our lives. People who have lived a disciplined life, such as those who have been in the military, or have been successful in sports, academia, or business have an advantage because they are already accustomed to making disciplined decisions, setting priorities and making sacrifices. Satan, our own carnal nature and the world around us will make sure there are ample weed seeds in our minds and hearts to keep us distracted from producing a full harvest. The corruption of sin at work in our humanity requires the application of spiritual disciplines to overcome. It is the only way we can live a life that honors God. Living a spiritually disciplined life is the only way we can move from being declared righteous at the moment of salvation to living the righteousness of Christ in our daily lives.

Acknowledge Truth

One of the best proactive things we can do for our spiritual health is to accept that the Bible is the standard of truth for our spiritual lives. It is the basis of our faith and practice. In 1 Timothy 3:16-17

Paul wrote, "All Scripture is God-breathed and is useful for teaching, rebuking, correcting and training in righteousness, so that the servant of God may be thoroughly equipped for every good work." In Paul's day, scripture consisted only of the 39 books we call the Old Testament. Those who believe the Old Testament has little value for us today, are mistaken. Christ is preached and revealed in those Old Testament scriptures. They were the Bible of the early church and it served them well.

We have an additional 27 books in our Bible today. They, too, are God-breathed and useful in our daily lives. While our society's view of the truth of scripture has changed a lot in the last 100 years, God's truth does not change,[1] nor is it dependent upon the whims of human ideology, comfort or human popularity. The Bible, both Old and New Testaments, is as reliable today as it was when each book was originally penned.

While various sciences may question the proclamations of the Bible, new discoveries in archeology, cosmology and other scientific disciplines continue to validate the testimony of the Bible. The Bible is first and foremost a book about our relationship with our Creator and His desire for us to know Him and be in right relationship with Him. It is not a scientific work, but where it speaks scientifically, it is correct. The conflict between science and scripture often comes from the way we interpret scientific facts. Modern culture tends to leap from known fact to popular speculation based on individual or cultural biases. In fact, many people today have made a religion out of science.

The Theory of Evolution is taught as a scientific fact in today's educational systems. The truth is that neither evolution nor creation can be concretely proven. Whatever we believe about our origin takes a significant amount of faith. If you have nagging questions about the beginning of the Bible when it says, "In the beginning, God created...,"[2] I encourage you to research the works of both creationists and evolutionists. Listen to the arguments on both sides of the discussion of human origins. Ask God to reveal His truth to you and make up your own mind. Many scientists have concluded that evolution cannot be true, even though they do not believe in a personal God as revealed in the Judeo-Christian scriptures and traditions. Other scientists believe science points to and supports the existence of the God of the Bible. Conduct your own search for truth and allow the Holy Spirit to speak to you. God is not threatened by our sincere questions in our quest for understanding truth.

As part of your effort to determine if God is, take a few evenings to get out in the country, or go to the beach, or desert, on a clear night. Be prepared to listen to your spirit, not just your mind and five senses. Look up at the stars and the vastness of Creation and let the testimony of God's creation speak to you. David proclaimed in Psalm 19:1-4, "The heavens declare the glory of God; the skies proclaim the work of his hands. Day after day they pour forth speech; night after night they reveal knowledge. They have no speech; they use no words; no sound is heard from them. Yet their voice goes out into all the earth, their words to the ends of the world." Ask God to show you his truth. Listen to your spirit. Listen for His Spirit. Paul wrote in Romans that God's power and eternal godhead can be known through the testimony of Creation.[3] If we listen, Creation will speak to us.

Another source of truth is universal knowledge. What I mean by that is that most religions contain something like the Golden Rule, "Treat others the way you would like them to treat you."[4] Such a truth is nearly universal, but it is not central to salvation in Christ. There are many universal truths that have been passed down in different cultures. Many have argued on this basis, that all religions are essentially the same.

Physical laws are also part of God's truth. We tend to put scientific knowledge in one bucket and God in another bucket. God is often categorized in the "religion" bucket and completely unrelated to scientific knowledge. However, if God is the Creator as revealed in the Bible, then it is humanity that is playing catch up on knowledge. Human beings are discovering new things all the time. Creator God has known everything we know and more since before any human being ever existed.

One short coming of physical science is that it looks at the physical world and declares universal "truth" from only a physical perspective. If we fail to recognize there is a spiritual aspect to human existence and define all of life from a purely physical perspective, then we miss out on the whole picture and our worldview is skewed. Conversely, we can do the same thing by looking at everything from only a spiritual perspective. If the God of the Bible exists, then Creation itself testifies of Him. We tend to think so highly of ourselves when we decode a complex scientific system. Yet, the God who created every system also has the power to override every system. Our view of God is such that we do not have room in our belief system for a being whom we cannot see to have known eons before we even existed all that we have discovered – and more. What puny thinking we often succumb to out of our drive to not need God.

While truth can be found in more places than the Bible, such as in nature and other religions, only the Bible proclaims the truth about how our Creator has dealt with our inherited inability to live in right relationship with Him. The Bible also shows the way for us to establish a personal relationship with our Creator based on grace through faith alone.[5] Only the Bible says that eternal life is not something we earn, but it is God's gift to those who believe in and trust Him.[6] Every other religion gives instruction on how we can try to appease god and maybe, possibly, have a chance at eternity in paradise. The message of the Bible is not wishy-washy but gets directly to the point and establishes a solid foundation of truth upon which we can base our lives.[7] No other system of knowledge adequately deals with the reality of our corrupted, human nature and offers a cure for that corruption. This biblical system of knowledge also offers us an eternal hope based on the actions of a loving Creator God toward humanity.

The Bible is the story of Creator God's interactions with one family that He chose to be His witness to all generations. It is God's story of redemption and His work to save human beings from the death and corruption that comes from rejecting a relationship with their Creator. Further, the Bible is the only collection of writings that tells us about Jesus, who is fully God and became fully human.[8] He lived as a servant and offered His life a ransom for the sins of the world.[9] He rose from the dead victorious over every ailment and opposition to the wellbeing of humanity.[10]

The first step, then, in growing in our life in Christ is to accept by faith that the Bible is God's communication to humans of the truth that will lead us to relationship with our Creator for this life and the life to come. People who do not have a solid grounding in truth can be swayed by nearly anything.[11] It is interesting to talk with people who have abandoned a system of faith and standards. Every new fad or idea is something to latch on to. Western culture's growing rejection of biblical truth in the last 100 years has brought us to a place where large sections of our culture are open to the final deception of the Antichrist. John wrote that the spirit of Antichrist was already around at the end of the first century.[12] It is even more prevalent today and will grow stronger. If the world is to become like it was in the days of Noah, as Jesus said it would,[13] then the world view of anti-Christ will become even more dominant in the world. It is likely that unless God moves in a new revival, the speed of culture toward a more dominant anti-Christ society will continue to increase.

Delusion will only grow stronger as we get closer to the return of Jesus Christ. Morality will continue to break down and the discarding of moral standards will become more normal in our culture than it is already. A greater reliance upon the physical, with its technological marvels, will grow as humanity abandons a reliance upon our Creator and Heavenly Father. Our uniqueness as Strangers will become more of a contrast as these things happen in our culture. Scriptures say the deception will be so great, that if it were possible, even the elect of God will be deceived.[14] Is it any wonder that philosophies around evolution, human superiority and the unlimited potential of humanity are gaining prominence in our world today?

Paul wrote to Timothy that he was to study to show himself a man ready to teach the Gospel.[15] To be sure, we need to be those who take the time to learn God's truth and apply it to our lives. God's truth is the only defense we have against every deception thrown at us.[16] God's truth provides a solid foundation for our lives, but it takes an exercise of will and consistent effort to grow spiritually. In time, with God's daily grace, we will have the strength to stand firm against the wiles of Satan, the draw of worldly living and the appeal of sin's corruption within us. God's truth is what we stand on. While accepting truth is essential, knowing the truth is not enough. We also need to know the One who is Truth.

Communion with God

Jesus said, "I am the Way, the Truth and the Life." To know Him is to have eternal life.[17] Therefore, in addition to understanding truth, we need to become more acquainted with God as a Person. That means we need to invest time building relationship with God. Through faith in Christ, we enjoy the gift of a personal relationship with Creator God. As with any relationship, we grow closer as we spend time with that person. Time in worship, prayer and quiet communion with God will cause us to take on more of the personhood of Jesus. The mission of the Holy Spirit is to conform us to the image of Jesus.[18] It is a work the Holy Spirit will be performing in us until our physical body ceases to function and we receive our glorified body.

Worship and praise help us focus our attention on God and be more open to His working in our lives. Worship is a place of presenting ourselves to God as instruments of right living.[19] We can worship God anywhere. It does not have to happen in a church gathering. I often will go for a long drive and play worship music, enjoying God's presence. However, it is a good idea not to lift your hands and close your eyes while driving! Worship can be anything from a few words at your desk at work, to a gathering of thousands singing in unison.

Another aspect of worship to consider is that how we live our lives is a form of worship. In Romans 12:1, Paul said that offering our bodies to God as living sacrifices is our, "true and proper worship." Choosing to follow God through faith in Christ, honors God and brings us into more intimate relationship with our Creator.

We frequently hear from God in the quiet times of our lives when we take the time to focus our spirit on Him and allow His Spirit to speak to us. All too often the voice of the Spirit is drowned out by all the noise of our modern lives. Radio, television, politics, the hustle bustle of life and concern over the struggles we face daily work to drown out the voice of the Holy Spirit as He encourages us and works to build us up in Christ. God promises that as we put Him as our highest priority in life, He will provide everything we need for daily living.[20] Setting aside time to quietly sit and reflect on God, giving to Him our concerns and rehearsing His promises can give us peace during life's storms.

There are times in our life as Strangers that God will give us grace for the moment. Sometimes our struggles are so intense, that we cannot think about tomorrow, or next week. Our pain or struggles can be such that all we see is right now. When we turn to God in those times, He will give us grace moment by moment, day by day to progress through the trials to a more productive place. God is the God of right now, as well as the God in whom we can trust for our future. He cares for you and me right now! He is here!

Prayer is another aspect of being in communion with God. It is in prayer that we lay our lives before God and ask His intervention in the areas of life in which we need His help and intercede for the needs of others. Prayer is often accompanied by fasting and meditation on God's word.

Disciplining our flesh to go without physical food to focus on seeking God is a powerful tool God has given us to grow in our spiritual awareness. Isaiah wrote that the purpose of fasting is to break bondage and to set the oppressed free.[21] Prayerfully mulling over, or meditating on, a passage of scripture that is particularly meaningful can be a deeply spiritual experience. It is a practice we need to include in our lives regularly if we want to grow spiritually.[22]

Many great books and devotional materials have been written that can give us more in-depth guidance on how to deepen our spiritual life in

Christ. The writings of believers throughout history can be a tremendous resource for cultivating fruit in our lives. The personal experiences of believers, both past and present, can give us a perspective outside our own cultural and generational biases and limitations.

Cultivating our relationship with God is a big part of doing the work that brings forth fruit in our lives. Getting God's truth in our hearts and minds requires an investment of time with God in study, prayer, praise, worship and meditation upon His truth. Small amounts of daily time devoted to these activities will bring forth more fruit than sporadic, longer investments of time. Consistency is as important as the quantity of time, perhaps more so. An investment of a half hour to an hour every day devoted to study, prayer and meditation can dramatically change our lives from the inside out over a period of years.

The fruit of the Spirit from Galatians 5:22-23 is not fruit that we suddenly decide we will live out one day. Like any fruit, the fruit of the Spirit grows from a bud, to a blossom, to a small fruit to a full fruit that satisfies. It is a process we do not control; it is God's process. However, our choices can facilitate or hinder the production of fruit. Choices. There's that word again.

There are times in our lives when we are faced with very tough choices. We may be tempted to walk away from God, or to do things we know are wrong just to get some sort of a break from the pressure we are feeling. I once heard a man who chose to commit adultery talk about the stop signs that God put in his way. He said that God put those stop signs in his life to prevent him from making a choice that would bring devastation to him and to his family. Rather than pay attention to what God was trying to tell him, he blew right through every stop sign God put in front of him. If he had paid attention to those stop signs, rather than ignore them, he would have saved himself and his family a lot of pain.

In those tough, or tempting, times of our lives, God will give us moments of grace to avoid making bad decisions that can lead to needless pain and suffering in our earthly life. It is crucial in those times to say, "Yes" to God's grace. Paul wrote that when we are in those times of temptation, God will provide a way to escape.[23] This is grace that God extends to us in love, not in judgment. He longs for us to make good decisions to move our lives in the right direction. In His direction.[24]

Serve Others

We are not saved for ourselves. While God loves us deeply as individuals, He did not create us to be self-serving and self-focused creatures. We are more than biological units responding to physical stimuli within physical boundaries. As we examined in chapter two, we are created in God's image with the ability to reason and have relationship on a spiritual level as well as a physical basis. God Himself is a Being of relationship. We are no less so. We need to be in relationship with one another to fulfill who we were designed to be and to gain strength in our spiritual uniqueness.

As Strangers in this world, God calls us to love one another and to submit to one another.[25] Through mutual sharing with fellow followers in Jesus, we encourage others to grow and are encouraged to endure hardships and persevere through our own doubts as well. We encourage each other in our faith by sharing experiences with other believers, enjoying the support of friendship and praying for one another.[26] Through expressing ourselves as part of God's family and allowing the Holy Spirit to work through us with other Strangers, we grow in the recognition of how we fit into God's Kingdom.

The writer of the letter to the Hebrews exhorts us to thoughtfully consider each other and encourage each other to do good works while remembering to assemble for worship and our mutual benefit.[27] It is through this fellowship with other believers that we see that we are not alone. We also see that many of the struggles we face in our experience as Strangers are common to all of us.[28] Paul instructed the Corinthians that, when they gather together, everything should be done orderly and for the building up of others, not our own glory.[29] Not all of us teach from the pulpit, but we can pray for one another and engage in meaningful conversation where we build each other up. Not all of us lead worship, but we can all offer an encouraging word to someone who is going through a rough time. Not all of us are called to plant churches, but we can all give a little of our financial resources to help make it possible.

Jesus gave us an example of servanthood when He washed the disciples' feet. He said His disciples should serve one another in the same way He served them.[30] That heart of service to others is to characterize the Stranger's life. Even when we are called to leadership, we are called to serve those whom we lead not to lord it over others.[31] Performing acts of service to the church based on our unique gifting is one way we can grow spiritually. Paul said to consider each other as more important than ourselves.[32] It is hard to get egotistical when you take on the attitude of a servant. Something as simple as being a greeter or usher in church services can work to break down the "me first" orientation we all are influenced by in our culture.

Beyond serving our fellow Strangers, volunteering at a local food bank, or mission to the homeless, or serving in our communities are also things we can do. Serving those in need shows us that most of us have a life we should not complain about. For most of us, life could be a lot worse. For most of us, our struggles pale when compared to many of those in need around us. We may not drive an expensive car, or live in a luxurious home, but we do have a lot to be thankful for that we often take for granted. Jesus came to serve and gave us the ultimate example in his life. He calls us to look beyond our own needs and bless others.

Serving others, whether in a spiritual capacity or a physical one, not only gets our eyes off ourselves, the service we give allows us to extend the love of Christ to others. When we allow God's Spirit to guide us in ways to serve, we often find ourselves in conversations and situations that are divine appointments. Divine appointments are times when God puts us in front of someone He would have us minister too. We might give an encouraging word, or simply pray for someone. It could also be something as simple as a warm smile to someone who feels forgotten and unloved. As we step out and extend a helping hand, we provide an avenue through which God can touch people with his presence in us and bring about changed lives through us.

Share Our Faith

In addition to serving others, God has called us to be witnesses to the world.[33] A natural outcome of serving others is having the opportunity to share our faith. Sharing our testimony with believers builds them up and lets us see how much we all have in common. Sharing our testimony with people who do not yet believe gives the Holy Spirit the opportunity to use our unique perspective and experience to reveal truth to the person listening. Even if we do not see a person come to faith as we are sharing, we are providing

150

the Holy Spirit with words to bring back to their hearts and minds to draw them to Christ. He will use everything we give Him.

I have heard the testimony of several people in my life who were impacted by my testimony but were led to the Lord by someone else. I got to plant seeds, or water seeds that someone else planted, but another person reaped the harvest when that person's faith reached the critical point.[34] The Holy Spirit orchestrated it all and many people played a part, including people who were simply praying for them. We need only be concerned about faithfully and genuinely sharing our faith, not pressing for results unless guided by the Spirit to do so. Sharing our faith is not a high-pressure sales job. On a deeper level, it is speaking spirit to spirit, working in cooperation with the Holy Spirit. When we watch a person come to faith in Christ, even partly because of something we have said or done, is a tremendous source of joy and encouragement.

Another benefit of sharing our testimony is that we learn how to refute objections. Living the Stranger's life is not easy. It is the hardest thing you are likely ever to do. What makes it hard is that people who do not believe in Christ do not understand that our life as Strangers is first a spiritual one. Our choices can often be in opposition to what seems logical. God does not always direct us in a way that those around us believe is sound. But as we obey the Holy Spirit's leading, we see how God can often use things that seem foolish to others to bring about good results for us. The simple act of following the Spirit's lead is also a form of sharing our faith. As we live our lives in front of others, what God is doing in us shines through. Our testimony is often the testimony of a life well lived, not a set of beliefs well spoken.[35]

We may be frustrated at times when we don't see results from our testimony, or fruit from all our struggles. One thing to keep in mind is that people see how we live - how we respond to life situations and challenges. They may not say anything about what they see in us, but they are watching us nonetheless. They notice as we grow and stand for what is right in God's eyes. How we live matters. It makes a difference and eventually we will hear from some people around us how our lives benefit them – how our lives make a difference in their lives.

In those moments, we get to recognize that our commitment to growth and our dedication to Christ really do mean something beyond ourselves. As we work at growing in the Lord, we will grow in our ability to share our faith. As we grow in our understanding of God's ways and learn to refute the objections of those in this world, we will see the certainty of God's truth more clearly. By God's grace, we will also see some of the people we talk with come to know their Creator and begin an eternity in relationship with Him.

Live by Faith

The life of the Stranger is a life lived by faith. Our struggle in this life with the corruption of sin and tactics of Satan is won by God's grace through faith as surely as we are saved by God's grace through faith.[36] We learn to have victory over Satan and recognize his devious ways through understanding truth and staying tuned in to God's Spirit within us.

The question that moved me to this study and to share it was, "How do we put to death the deeds of the body?" Of all the principles I reviewed in my studies, faith is the most crucial element. Faith is to our spiritual life what breathing is to our physical life. Everything in this chapter, in fact, in the book, has an underpinning of faith. Without faith, none of our actions will result in the growth we desire. In fact, "It's impossible to please God apart from faith. And why? Because anyone who wants to approach God must believe both that he exists and that he cares enough to respond to those who seek him."[37]

The heart of the answer I was seeking when I started this study is found in Romans 6:11 where he wrote, "From now on, think of it this way: Sin speaks a dead language that means nothing to you; God speaks your mother tongue and you hang on every word. You are dead to sin and alive to God. That's what Jesus did" (The Message). We put to death the deeds of the flesh first by recognizing that the work of Jesus on the cross did far more than secure salvation for us, it crucified the corrupt nature within us. His death purchased ultimate victory for us.

Stop and reflect on this truth for a moment. What Paul is saying is that everything within us that would draw us away from God was nailed to the cross with Jesus. We will not see the influence of that corrupt nature completely cut off until this body of corruption dies, but we have a weapon to fight against the draw of sin within us that we apply it to our daily lives. It is God's truth applied by faith. When we live in the acknowledgement of the truth of Romans 6:11, we will see more victory than if we fail to proactively apply the truth to our daily lives. We have all often heard this verse from Galatians 5:16, "I say then: Walk in the Spirit and you shall not fulfill the lust of the flesh" (NKJV). The Message puts it this way. "My counsel is this: Live freely, animated and motivated by God's Spirit. Then you won't feed the compulsions of selfishness." Christ has set us free from the lists of dos and don'ts. Living in daily relationship with God's Spirit within us is the only way to victory. The Stranger's life, then, is a life of learning to follow God's Holy Spirit within us.

Believing what Christ did for us is the beginning. Everything above in this chapter comes after believing the truth of Jesus' sacrifice and resurrection. I left faith for last because it needs to be the paramount thing in our minds. Living by faith is a choice we Strangers make every day. What we do is important and faith without works is not real faith, but the Stranger's work begins

154

with believing God. We walk in the Spirit when we apply God's truth to our lives by faith and live in the freedom He has purchased for us. The Stranger's life is not adhering to a compilation of rules. That is religion and it leads to living a life that is not alive with the Spirit. The Stranger's life is a life lived pursuing God in the freedom of fellowship with the Holy Spirit. The challenge is to live continuously in that freedom and not get sucked back into the bondage of our former life.

God's direction comes first through His word; second, through relationship with Him; third, through understanding who we are made to be and how God wants to use us in His Kingdom and; fourth, through wise counsel and exercising of spiritual gifts among other believers. Faith applies to every area of a Stranger's life. Faith relates to the Stranger's conflict in the fact that victory is won by employing faith. Revelation 12:11 says of those who overcame Satan that they did it by the blood of the Lamb and the word of their testimony. We trust God's Word. We trust in the sufficiency of Christ's shedding of blood that brought about His death and His resurrection to bring us not only eternal life, but victory over Satan, sin and our own corrupt desires.

Paul's command to "crucify the flesh",[37] or to "put to death the deeds of the body,"[38] is not a call to a self-debasing, nor are they a masochistic approach to life. Crucifying the flesh is applying God's truth to our lives by faith and being disciplined to live in a way that fosters our spiritual

155

growth in Christ. By seeing ourselves as those whom Christ has delivered from sin and daily seeking God's grace and mercy for our failures, we can live each day of our lives in God's peace, presence and strength.

Final Thoughts

The bottom-line questions of the conflict we face as Strangers are these: Will we choose to continue to acknowledge that God is? Will we choose to continue to acknowledge Him as Creator? Will we choose to continue to live as though we need Him?

Our inherited, corrupt, human nature fights against those choices all the time. We face this conflict on a personal and individual level, but we also face it as societies and ultimately as the entire family of humanity. By consistently choosing to engage in the actions that foster our spiritual growth, we will gain a greater awareness of the presence and work of God in our lives and we will grow in our fruitfulness for our Creator. The stronger we are in our spiritual life with Christ, the more likely it is that we will avoid the pitfalls of the Pharisees, the crowds and the disciples.

In his letter to the Ephesians, Paul wrote about our need to take on the full armor of God because our battle is not a physical one but a battle against spiritual powers. The armor is a vivid picture of a personal battle – a conflict if you will.

The original reader would have pictured a Roman soldier outfitted for battle. The armor consists of truth around our waist, a breastplate of righteousness, feet that are shod with the preparation of the gospel of peace, the shield of faith, the helmet of salvation and a sword, which is the word of God.[39] We are outfitted with the spiritual armor as we grow in Christ. His Spirit within us will build us up to be a unique warrior in His service as we follow Him in this life.

There is grace for when we fall short and fail as we all do at times.[40] But the abundant availability of God's grace is never a license to sin nor is it intended to provide an excuse for failing to live holy life.[41] Neither is God's call to holiness an authorization to judge people, or set ourselves up as superior to anyone.[42] If we will apply God's truth to our lives with sincerity and consistency, when our days on this planet end, we can say with Paul, "I have fought the good fight, I have finished the race, I have kept the faith. Now there is in store for me the crown of righteousness, which the Lord, the righteous Judge, will award to me on that day — and not only to me, but also to all who have longed for his appearing."[43]

Many believers at times, including me, tend to take this conflict in which are engaged too lightly – or approach it too passively. We have the power in Christ, through His Spirit, to overcome. The forces that oppose us are militant in their approach to us. If we better understood what we have been given and the seriousness of the conflict,

157

perhaps we too would be more militant in our personal struggles. The option is available for us to embrace this life with faith and engage with God in living in such a way that we will move into eternity with God and impact the lives of others along the way. This is the Stranger's choice.

May God's grace and peace be with you as you navigate your own Stanger's conflict and usher you home when your ambassadorship[44] here is complete.

To check for updates and new material by the author, go to www.thestrangerslife.com

About the Author

Brad grew up on a small farm in Oregon. Farm life gave him the opportunity to learn hard work and come to enjoy solitude. As the youngest of three siblings, Brad was the only child in the home from about the age of 12 till he left home at 19. The family moved to Eugene after Brad graduated from high school. Two years later, Brad moved to Portland to begin working at an electronics firm.

Brad first came to faith in Christ at the age of six. It is a decision he has reaffirmed multiple times in his life. At 23 years of age, God called him to attend Bible college in Los Angeles, California. There, he earned a BA in Bible with a minor in biblical languages.

After college, Brad went to work as a model and mold maker in the golf club industry. For nine years, he developed his skills and eventually started a business with his college friend, Rick. When the industry changed, and the work went overseas, Brad decided it was time to move back to Oregon.

Back in the Portland area, Brad went to work for an international distribution company. He was promoted to warehouse manager in a short time. Brad went back to school in 1999, obtained a BS in business management, and eventually became a regional operations coordinator. He helped develop and manage four service-oriented facilities from Oregon to Minnesota. As a leader, problem solver, trainer, and technical writer, Brad's work was recognized as contributing to world class business operations that were modeled in various facilities in the organization.

Through the years, Brad's faith in Jesus Christ has been an anchor in his life. Though never involved in ministry professionally, Brad's interest in and love for scripture has not lessened. In the more than 30 years since Bible college, he has taught Sunday School, led Bible studies, developed teachings for house church settings, and held fast to faith in Christ.

Brad desires to share what God has worked into him through life's struggles, trials, and successes. One way he has discovered the joy of sharing is through writing. The Stranger's Conflict is his first book and was published in 2017. More information about the Stranger's theme and Brad's weekly blog can be found at www.thestrangerslife.com.

Notes

❧

INTRODUCTION
1. Romans 7:15
2. Hebrews 11:13
3. 2 Corinthians 5:20

CHAPTER 1
1. Matthew 7:7
2. John 7:11
3. John 7:14
4. Mark 7:8
5. Mark 7:13
6. John 7:16-17
7. Matthew 12:2
8. Genesis 2:2
9. Exodus 2:8-11
10. Exodus 16:1-8
11. Matthew 12:10
12. Matthew 12:11-12
13. Matthew 12:8
14. John 3:1-2
15. John 8:51
16. John 8:39
17. John 8:52-53, 57
18. John 8:59
19. Micah 5:2
20. Matt. 23:27-28
21. John 6:1-2
22. John 6:5-7

23.   John 6:9-11

24.   John 6:14

25.   John 6:15

26.   John 6:25-26

27.   John 6:27

28.   John 6:32-34

29.   John 6:35-59

30.   John 6:66

31.   John 6:67-69

32.   Mark 1:9

33.   Luke 9:29

34.   Mark 9:3

35.   Luke 9:30-31

36.   Mark 9:5-8; Luke 9:33-36

37.   Luke 9:1-6

38.   Mark 9:14

39.   Mark 9:15

40.   Mark 9:16-18; 29

41.   Philippians 2:5-11

CHAPTER 2

1.   Matthew 28:19

2.   Genesis 1:2

3.   Revelation 3:6

4.   Numbers 11:24-25

5.   Judges 6:11-12; 34

6.   1 Samuel 1:24-28

7.   1 Samuel 10:10; 11:6

8.   1 Samuel 16:13

9.   1 Samuel 16:14

10.   Ezra 6:13-18

11.   John 4:24

12.   John 20:22

13.   John 15:26

14.   Luke 23:46

15.   Acts 7:59

16.   1 Corinthians 2:10-14

17.   Acts 7:55; Romans 8:34; Ephesians 1:20; Colossians 3:1

18.   Matthew 22:37-40 NIV

19.   Genesis 1:31

CHAPTER 3

1.   Genesis 2:15-17

2.   Genesis 3:2-3

3.   Gen. 1:31

4.   Genesis 3:5

5.   1 Tim 2:14

6.   Isaiah 14:12-15; Ezekiel 28:12-19;

7.   Luke 10:18; Revelation 12:3-4,9

8.   John 8:44

9.   2 Corinthians 11:14

10.   1 John 4:16

CHAPTER 4

1.   Genesis 6:5

2.   Genesis 8:21

3.   Genesis 9:13-17

4.   Genesis 12:1-3

5.   Genesis 15:6

6.   Genesis 15:4-5; 17:1-8

7.   Genesis 16:1-4

8.   Genesis 21:9-13

9.   Genesis 21:1-7

10.   Genesis 25:24-26

11.   Genesis 37:4,18-28

12.   Genesis 39:20-23

13.   Genesis 41:14-36

14.   Genesis 46:26

15.   Genesis 15:13

16.   Exodus 1:8-14

17.   Exodus 3:10

18.   Exodus 12: 31-42

19.   Exodus 6:8

20.   Numbers 13:31-14:4

21.   Numbers 14:28-30

22.   Numbers 14:11

23.   Judges 2:20-3:6

24.   Judges 21:25

25.   1 Samuel 8:1-4

26.   1 Samuel 8:7

27.   1Samuel 9:17

28.   1Samuel 9:1-2

29.   1Samuel 13:1-14

30.   2 Samuel 11:1-27

31.   1 Samuel 15:12

32.   1 Samuel 15:2-3

33.   1 Samuel 15:9

34.   1 Samuel 15:18-21

35.   1 Samuel 15: 23,28

36.   1 Samuel 15:30

37.   2 Samuel 6:13-14

38.   2 Samuel 24:18-24

39.   1 Chronicles 22:8

40.   1 Chronicles 22:9

41.   1 Chronicles 22:2-5

42.   1 Kings 11:4-13

43.   1 Kings 12:4

44.   1 Kings 3:5-15

45.	1 Kings 4:29-30
46.	1 Kings 12:14
47.	1 Kings 12:20-21
48.	1Kings 12:28-33
49.	II Chronicles 33:9
50.	Deuteronomy 31:28-29
51.	1 Samuel 8:7
52.	Galatians 3:24
53.	Galatians 3:21

CHAPTER 5

1.	Romans 2:11
2.	Romans 3:19
3.	Ezekiel 18:20
4.	Genesis 8:5
5.	Genesis 9:21-23
6.	Hebrews 11:19
7.	Genesis 22:13
8.	John 3:16-17
9.	Genesis 35:9-15
10.	Exodus 1:8-14
11.	Exodus 12:1-13
12.	Exodus 12:14
13.	1 John 2:2
14.	Exodus 12:5
15.	Leviticus 17:11
16.	Matthew 5:17
17.	Hebrews 10:2-3
18.	Hebrews 10:12
19.	1 Peter 3:18
20.	Romans 3:25; 1 John 2:2, 4:10
21.	Romans 8:38-39

22.   Romans 10:8-10

CHAPTER 6

1.   2 Corinthians 13:14
2.   Ephesians 2:6
3.   1 Corinthians 12:20,27; Colossians 3:1-3
4.   Ephesians 1:13-14
5.   Philippians 2:12
6.   Ephesians 3:10
7.   Mark 4:4,14
8.   Mark 4:5-6, 16-17
9.   Mark 4:7, 18-19
10.   Mark 4:9, 20
11.   1 Corinthians 15:42-49
12.   1 Corinthians 13:12
13.   1 Corinthians 15:20-23

CHAPTER 7

1.   John 8:44
2.   John 10:10
3.   John 16:11
4.   Colossians 2:14-15
5.   1 John 4:8
6.   Romans 3:26
7.   Hebrews 4:9,16
8.   Matthew 11:28-30
9.   2 Timothy 2:8-10
10.   1 Corinthians 3:16
11.   Ephesians 1:5; Galatians 4:5
12.   John 3:16
13.   Matthew 25:46

14.   1 Corinthians 13:12

15.   1 Corinthians 15:52-54; 2 Corinthians 5:1-5

16.   1 Timothy 2:4

17.   Matthew 25:41

18.   Luke 4:5-6

19.   "For Him Who Has Ears To Hear," album. Released May 20, 1977, produced by Bill Maxwell and Keith Green

20.   John 16:28

21.   John 5:19; 6:38; 14:31

22.   Matthew 27:46

23.   Romans 3:24-26

24.   Ex. 6:7; Lev. 26:12; Jer. 30:22

25.   1 Timothy 2:4

26.   Mark 8:34; Revelation 22:17

27.   James 4:8

28.   Psalm 116:15

CHAPTER 8

1.   1 Corinthians 2:14

2.   Numbers 22:28-31

3.   Exodus 3:1-5ff

4.   Acts 8:8-11

5.   Acts 8:12-13

6.   Acts 8:14-17

7.   Acts 8:18-19

8.   Acts 8:20-23

9.   Acts 8:10

10.   Acts 8:6-7

11.   Acts 8:8

12.   Galatians 5:19-21

13.   Galatians 5:22

14.   Matthew 6:33

15.   Matthew 16:24
16.   Matthew 11:29-30
17.   1 John 1:8
18.   Prov. 4:23
19.   1 Tim 4:16

CHAPTER 9

1.   Matthew 27:18
2.   Matthew 27:20-26
3.   John 12:19
4.   Matthew 7:28-29; John 7:46
5.   Isaiah 61:1-3; Luke 4:18-22
6.   John 8:42
7.   1 Samuel 15:22
8.   John 3:1-21; 7:50-51
9.   John 6:51-54
10.   Luke 22:19-20
11.   Luke 22:20
12.   1 Corinthians 5:7; Hebrews 10:5-10
13.   John 6:15
14.   1 Corinthians 2:14
15.   John 6:63
16.   Luke 9:1-6
17.   Luke 9:41
18.   Acts 4:18-22

CHAPTER 10

1.   Hebrews 13:8
2.   Genesis 1:1
3.   Romans 1:20
4.   Matthew 7:12
5.   Ephesians 2:8-9
6.   John 3:16; Romans 6:23

7. Matthew 7:24-27
8. John 1:14; Philippians 2:6-8
9. 1 Timothy 2:6
10. 1 Corinthians 15:55-57
11. Ephesians 4:14
12. 1 John 4:3
13. Matthew 24:37
14. Matt. 24:24
15. 2 Tim 2:15
16. Ephesians 4:14-24
17. John 14:6
18. Romans 8:29
19. Romans 6:13
20. Matthew 6:33
21. Isaiah 58:6-7
22. Psalms 19:14
23. 1 Corinthians 10:13
24. James 4:8
25. John 13:34; Ephesians 5:21; Romans 12:10
26. 2 Corinthians 1:3-5
27. Hebrews 10:24-35
28. 1 Corinthians 10:13
29. 1 Corinthians 14:26
30. John 13:12-15
31. Matthew 20:25-28
32. Philippians 2:3
33. Acts 1:8
34. 1 Corinthians 3:6-7
35. 2 Corinthians 3:1-3
36. Ephesians 2:8-9
37. Hebrews 11:6, The Message)
38. Galatians 5:24
39. Romans 8:13; Colossians 3:5

40. Ephesians 6:10-18
41. 1 John 1:9
42. Romans 6:1-2;15-16
43. Matthew 7:1; Romans 14:4
44. 2 Timothy 4:7-8
45. 2 Cor. 5:20

Made in the USA
Middletown, DE
23 June 2019